Green Two

"Sgt. Dennis Noble"

'One of Churchill's Few.'

By
Keith Arnold

Southern Counties
Aviation Research/Publications

First Published in Great Britain January 2003
By Southern Counties Aviation Research/Publications.
PO Box 334
Chichester
PO20 2XJ

ISBN number 0-9544141-0-1
Printed and bound by Antony Rowe Ltd, Eastbourne

CONTENTS.

****

“*WARNING*”.

The Text on pages 54 & 55
Explain Graphic Details that may
Cause Distress.

PHOTOGRAPHS.

Illustrations.

The Author and Publisher.
Apologise for any distress caused by
Photographs and Written Material printed in this book
That may offend. Care and consideration has been upheld where possible.

FOREWORD
By
One of the Few 1940.
Group Captain Thomas Fredrick Dalton-Morgan
DFC +Bar. DSO. OBM.

There are not many narrative accounts of our gallant sergeant pilots who fought and died in the Battle of Britain.
This is the story of one such pilot Sgt Dennis Noble who had always wanted to fly so he joined the Royal Air Force Volunteer Reserve.
After only a few hours flying experience on Hurricanes he was posted to 43 Squadron Tangmere, where he joined my flight, as a much needed replacement.
Before flying him on operations we endeavored to give him as with all our replacements our experience on how to use his aircraft tactically in combat, with the demands of operations this was always Insufficient. On one of his early sorties he destroyed his first enemy aircraft, but shortly afterwards he was shot down and killed.
He was found still in his crashed aircraft some fifty-six years later.
Unfortunately his was a short war as it was for many other gallant young men. "We will remember them".

The story also mentions two other gallant former Sergeant pilots of 43 Squadron they were later commissioned and survived the war – Group Captain Frank Carey DSO.DFC.DFM also Jim Hallowes DFC. DFM.
Keith Arnold has written a memorable story, & I am honored to add my tribute.

Tom Dalton-Morgan
Flight Commander of 43 Squadron 'B' Flight 1940.
Longest Commanding officer of 43 Squadron to date.

Group Captain ***Thomas Fredrick Dalton-Morgan***
DSO. OBE. DFC. B Sc. BE.
Commanding Officer of 43 Squadron September – December 1940.

Born on 23rd March 1917 in Cardiff, he joined the RAF on a short service commission in August 1935. After his training at 11FTS at Wittering he was posted to 22 Squadron flying Vickers Vildebeeste torpedo-bombers at Donibristle. After a short stay with the air ministry in May 1939 In June 1940 he was posted operational as Flight commander of 'B' flight 43 Squadron at Tangmere Sussex. Tom Dalton – Morgan was an experienced fighter pilot & a true leader to all those fortunate enough to be taken under his wing. As a young replacement pilot straight out of training school, Sgt Dennis Noble was observed & taught new skills by Tom Morgan & Squadron Leader George Lott another experienced pilot who also cared about the lack of combat knowledge these youngsters had. Maybe their teaching skills of battle tactics saved or prolonged lives to some extent during those complex few months of the war. Tom was wounded by crossfire during a battle with German Heinkel IIIs on the 13th August 1940 whilst flying Hurricane P3972 but nothing could keep him away from his comrades & the chance of repelling German raiders constantly attacking his Country. September 6th 1940 bought him bad luck once again when he was shot down after combat with Bf 109s flying as Blue 1 leader of 'B' flight. His combat report states; "I attacked one Me 109 from behind and gave it one long burst. An explosion occurred in the port main plane and the aircraft commenced a steep dive towards the west issuing black smoke, I later saw it and three other aircraft crash into the sea 9 miles off Dungeness. I presumed that the two other aircraft had to be those shot down by P/O Gorrie and Sgt Hurry. I climbed again and attacked another Me 109 proceeding in a southerly direction after one long burst I noticed damage to the wings and broke away as I saw it

Dive steeply I did not see this aircraft again. As I climbed & turned to regain my position I was hit by an aircraft diving out of the sun". Some years later Tom recollects the incident;
"As I recall there is not much to say leading up to my being shot up after take-off, I climbed away East towards Dungeness. Eventually I sighted a gaggle of Me 109s high above me. I realized that it was to late to engage them on the way in so I climbed to get into a position to intercept them on the way out. It gave me a nasty turn I can tell you when the instrument panel started falling apart & there was a disturbing bang as a shell exploded somewhere near me, the windscreen became difficult to see through. I really never saw the aircraft that hit me, but I did see his quick shadow as he crossed the sun but that was all. He was a pretty good shot because at the time I was hit I was in what I thought to be a tight climbing turn, needless to say I found I could turn much tighter when encouraged by a burst from a 10, this was a case of over confidence on my part I was lucky to have survived". Meanwhile back on the ground Toms maintenance crew comprising of Bill Littlemore engine mechanic & Tommy Poole Rigger had discovered that their heroic pilot had been shot up, as the stern voice of chiefly savage shouted 'stand by' the flight commander is returning. Bill & Tommy watched as Tom Morgan approached the aerodrome in FT-G, on landing it was soon evident that he had seen action the gun ports were exposed as the fabric patches flapped in the wind. There were cannon shell holes down the starboard side just behind the cockpit & right down to the tail, also the wind screen damage top left hand corner of its mounting former. Tom Dalton-Morgan was struggling in the cockpit his oxygen mask & microphone unclipped his face streaming with blood, he then looked out of his cockpit to get some idea of his direction as he couldn't see through the windscreen. Bill remembers screaming to Tommy Poole 'get the doc' as he climbed onto the starboard wing then helped his pilot out to safety.

Tom Morgan also had the miss fortune of coming down into the sea on the 24th July 1941, he takes up the story "*As a prelude to the story we had one of the first fighter dinghies ever under test in the squadron we were told by sector HQ Turnhouse, that an intelligence interception had been received that a Dornier was expected in the vicinity of St Abbs & would we arranged to intercept. I thought it a good opportunity to blood some of the new pilots, so I arranged as I remember three standing patrols comprising of an experienced leader & two new pilots. I took P/O Tafnell a new pilot as a back up on patrol it was also my turn to fly with the dingy as it happened. Tafnell & I were steaming along the coast at St Abbs Head at sea level the other patrols were seaward & out of sight. As back up we did not expect to see anything the weather was fine but hazy, to say the least I was surprised to see a Dornier 18 flying towards me from 9 o'clock at sea level it probably saw us at the same timeas it turn away through 180 degrees. Taffy & I pulled the plug & climbed towards the Dornier so that we could carry out a climbing attack from the rear starboard quarter, as we started our attack from out of range from about 5000 ft there were formidable grouching noises from my engine & the prop stopped. I carried on the attack followed by Taffy & we knocked the Dornier down. I told Taffy that I would have to ditch & to climb & give a Mayday over my position. I ditched & climbed out into the water & operated the co2 bottle of the dinghy, it was empty so I had to use the hand bellows managing to get some air into the dinghy. So there I was with a broken lower jaw where my face had hit the gun sight on ditching in a partially inflated dinghy feet out of the water head out of the water supported by my Mae West & my body in the water. For the rest of that day squadron aircraft searched for me I saw them but they did not see me then just before dark P/O Roy Du-Vivier & Joe Pippa saw me Joe flew over me at about 200 feet & through out his Mae West up wind of me, I eventually picked it up so that was dear old Joe he was such a good pilot that when he used to*

To fly in close formation with me he would touch the edge of my wing tip with the edge of his & once there was a dent in my wing tip to prove it. As the sea became rougher I spotted some of the crew from the Dornier in their dinghy I knew this because when I floated to the top of a wave I saw them about a mile East, but I am not sure if they saw me. Eventually I was picked up by HMS Ludlow & I told the officer in command about the German Crew but the vessal had to rejoin the convoy from which it had been diverted. After rescuing me the destroyer continued up the east coast and at various points e.g. Hull, Newcastle & the Firth of Forth a RAF air-sea rescue craft was sent out to intercept the destroyer & take me off. I gather just about the time a navel septic thought he would have to operate on me on board or I would go rotten. The Destroyer intercepted a small fishing smack bound for Aberdeen & I was transferred to the latter, bound up in a hammock & laid on the deck as they could not get me through the hatch to take me below. On route to Aberdeen the fishing boat was bombed & machine-gunned the skipper received a wound in the arm. Eventually on our arrival I was transferred to King Seat Navel Hospital. W/Com Eeles the station commander at Drem remarked on the accident 24th July 41 "I have no comments to make other than I consider this to be a classic example of how a first class pilot can attack an enemy aircraft while his engine is failing, shoot it down & then force land into the sea & get away with it".

Tom Commanded what became known as the Ibsley wing consisting of four Spitfire Sqdns two Typhoon Sqdns & two Canadian Mustang Sqdns also two Whirlwind Sqdns under his command they supported a preliminary landing on the Channel Islands.

Tom remained in Germany after the war attached to the 2nd Tactical Air Force & received the O.B.E June 1945. He was very active within N.A.T.O but retired to Australia as a Sheep farmer where Tom & his dearly loved wife Dee have raised a family, they now both enjoy retirement commuting between Australia & England.

Picture taken at Drem 1941.
Left to Right rear row: -
Squadron Leader Thomas Dalton-Morgan DSO.DFC.OBE.
P/O Roy Harries. Assistant Intelligence Officer. Two American Eagle Squadron Pilots.
Front Row Sgt Wilkinson Australian & Sgt Joe Pippa.

This picture is of Pilot Officer Ray Harries standing next to Squadron Leader Tom Dalton-Morgan's Hurricane his was the only aircraft in 43Squadron with the fighting cock in the strike position they were painted on the cowlings both sides from a drawing he gave to a little W.A.A.F artist in the parachute section. Tom still has the two panels.

MURMERS OF AN AIRFIELD.

For just one moment imagine standing in a field of freshly cut grass, the morning mist drifts slowly between the structures of buildings that once played a vital part in the quest for England's survival. A farmer waits eagerly for the morning sun to rise, so that yesterday's mown grass can be turned for haymaking. The enchanting chorus of the skylark replacing the once throbbing Rolls-Royce Merlin's of the Hurricanes & Spitfires hastily being prepared for another day's activities. 'Ghostly' shadows lurk harmlessly over the field once bustling with RAF personnel hastily carrying out their duties. Savour the peace & tranquillity of this forgotten aerodrome for a short while & let your mind wonder back to June 1940. The Battle of Britain is about to commence in earnest. As the mist clears we can expect to hear the 'Toll of the Airfield Bell' & that famous battle cry 'Scramble' echoing throughout dispersal areas. Its Tangmere 1940, a Pilot runs to his awaiting aircraft, struggling to get into his parachute, an eagerly awaiting ground crew help him into the cockpit, then a raised hand from the pilot indicates to his ground crew 'chocks away,' the squadron soon becomes Airborne & sets course towards Enemy Bombers attacking a British Convoy in the English Channel. Sadly some pilots may not return, & others wounded may have to fend for themselves & hope the horrors of fire, would not become reality, as their aircraft plummets earthwards, for one small moment their maybe time to take to the silk. Many were only young men in there twenties fighting for survival & their lives. "Is all this now forgotten?" In the immortal words of Sir Winston Churchill '***Never in the Field of Human conflict has so Much been Owed by so Many to so Few"*** A true inspiring account summing up the deeds bestowed upon the nation by these brave pilots & ground personnel working tirelessly keeping the machines of war airworthy. Defending the aerodrome & making sure that returning planes had somewhere to land, Battle weary & tired ammunition spent & fuel gauges reading empty, they return home to base.

This was home 'Well' as near as one could be to the comforts of family life, this field where 2500 young men & women saw action, some lived to tell the tales of heroism & sacrifice made during the months between July to October 1940, without them we would not be enjoying the democratic life style of today's society.

This book pays tribute to one of the Few who paid with his life trying to beat off an attack by the German Luftwaffe during August 1940. He was just an ordinary young man & like most people planning his future, regrettably he was called upon to defend his country. Originating from Retford Nottinghamshire, this young man had only one ambition to follow in the footsteps of his heroes, the Flying Ace's of World War One, such as Edward Mannock & Captain Roy Brown. He was also a very gifted Electrical Engineer with ideas that could have made him very prosperous in later years had he survived the onslaught of war in 1939. This young flyer was Sgt Dennis Noble destined to survive only twenty-seven day's on active service with 43 squadron Tangmere Sussex.

He was shot down and killed 30th August 1940, his Hurricane P3179 was recovered from the residential street of Woodhouse Road, Hove, Sussex during 1996 by the **Southern Counties Aviation Club.** During this operation Sgt Nobles remains were discovered still in the cockpit of his Hurricane, instantly gaining public sympathy & inspiration through the power of Television & Press. Questions needed to be answered 'How or why' was he left undiscovered since 1940, & just 'Who or What' had been laid to rest in the town cemetery of Retford 1940 after receiving full military honours. Quoting a phrase from a letter sent to his parents just after his death ***(Out of the Strain of the Doing & into the Peace of the Done)*** which sums up the tributes paid to him.

A remarkable modern residential apartment complex appropriately designated **Noble Court** commemorates him. Taking pride of place next to the crash site, a proud reminder for us all to gain inspiration from the deeds of one of the Few.

Dennis Noble age 17

Sister Phyllis in 1956.

Harry & Annie Noble

Three Generations of the Noble family.
Left to Right. Sister Phyllis, Dennis's Father Harry, Grandmother, Aunt standing. Mother Annie, Dennis age 8 and his brother John

THE COMFORTS OF HOME.

The Signing of the Armistice ending the First World War between the Allies & Germany on November 11 1918, signified a moment in time that would be reserved as a Day of Remembrance for everyone to reflect upon the Human sacrifice wasted by Countries at war. Who could predict that seventy-eight years later & after another World War, one of England's soldier's would be discovered & returned to the peace & tranquillity of his home. Two years after WW1 in the small market town of Retford, Nottinghamshire, Harry & Annie Noble gave birth to their third child, Dennis on 27th January 1920. It was at Hallcroft Road Retford that he spent his childhood with his sister Phyllis & elder brother John. Dennis was part of a well-united family giving love & support to especially each other, through the depression of the 1930s when the struggle to find work & lack of income, reared its ugly head in many families, but fortunately, the Nobles were survivors. Dennis put great faith in his sister, trusting her judgments & advice, He continued placing his trust in Phyllis & well into later years wrote many letters to her whilst on active service with the RAF. His father Harry Noble was a gentle & quiet man who loved to grow roses to high standards, winning prizes for his blooms at local flower shows. A Religious man who gave his family the chance to worship at the West Retford Baptist Church where Dennis spent one afternoon per week at Sunday school, He attended the Methodist day school throughout the week finally transferring to the Fredrick Milliner School. Dennis was a shy young man & did not appear to have many friends. He kept himself in his own world of entertainment, as he loved to make model aeroplanes, he made these out of wood & anything he could lay his hands that he could improvise giving him the first aspirations towards Aviation. One fine autumn afternoon in 1933, his attentions were drawn to the real aspects of flight as he noticed a biplane from a Barn Stormers Team performing aerobatics overhead. This gave him all the inspiration that a young teenager needed to plan a future in aviation. Dennis was bewildered by what he saw that day; he just had to make flying his achievement in life. He had grown up to respect the circumstances surrounding the poverty & hardship of the 1930s depression. To be successful he had to first escape the scenario of unemployment facing the Country. All his energy must therefore be placed into doing what he loved best. One activity he was fond of was the Boys Brigade & perhaps the closeness of being a part of what resembled life in the Services, inspired him to join the RAF. In his mind, he only thought of flying but would never have dreamt that it would be for his Country & his life in yet another War. If he could achieve high marks in the Boys Brigade & prove that he was capable, his future would be assured. During an interview with Keith Arnold *(Author)* his sister in law **Annie Evans,** originally married to John Noble spoke of Dennis as a shy young man *"I first met Dennis when he was fifteen years old, a quiet boy the only one living at home with his parents. A likable chap with whom I, as a newcomer to his family felt at home. His mother kept a watchful eye on his health as she regarded him as being of a nervous disposition, & she regularly administered doses of tonic"*. **Ken Lowe** another of his friends served with him at 6 O.T.U & later at Tangmere, confirmed the fact that Dennis was of a nervous disposition something I believe to be of importance when faced with the dramatic test of battle maybe one contribution towards his death! *"On our first meeting I found Dennis to be very drawn in fact shy, but nevertheless friendly & interesting, he could sometimes be very moody but didn't trouble anyone, he just retired to his bunk. He was a very close friend to me & a part of me died with him". (Ken Lowe)*

As a young man leaving school Dennis had found another interest, he discovered that friends were asking him to repair their broken radios & other electrical items. (Was this a new way forward)? In an old shed at the bottom of his father's garden, he persistently struggled with the many wires, valves & other components of old 1920s radios. This old shed survived until 1998, still bearing

the labels of radio parts he stored there. Some of Dennis's tools are still in circulation throughout the family, such as his hand-drill, now in the possession of his Nephew **Denis Noble Junior**. His newly found interest in the workings of radios helped, now that he was starting work at Curry's the electrical retailers in Retford, an old & well-established firm. It was not long though before he transferred to London where he stayed with his brother John & wife Annie she recalls *"Dennis subsequently left home to work at another branch of Curry's & stayed with us at Torbay Road, Rayners Lane South London, Staying upwards of a year before moving closer to his work he called to see us one day dressed in RAF uniform & took us by surprise. We always had expected that perhaps this would be his choice of forces, as he had always been interested in aeroplanes. 'However,' when his mother told us that he had gained his wings, astonishment was more of a surprise as we thought that ground crew would be all he would achieve".*
Before joining the RAF, Dennis decided to gain more experience working with radio apparatus, manufactured by Master Radio Ltd, of 1, Newton Road, High Holborn, WC2. His capabilities were proved, when he applied for a British Patent No 23534/39, covering the power supply of an Electric Shaver, he had designed. This device was an inverter boosting a 12-volt electrical supply, into 50-260 volts AC current.
The reason behind this extraordinary device was that he could not master the art of shaving, using a wet blade razor.
Owing to the fact that he spent most of his weekends travelling to & from Redhill, Aerodrome in Surrey, for his flying training, his device enabled him to shave from the comforts of his own car. Although very cumbersome compared to today's technology, it comprised of a square wooden box with carrying strap, & rather a large circuit of wiring and resisters. The Specification states, *"A device that enables such razors to be used where only a small voltage is obtainable & has a chief object to provide means, whereby such razors can be operated from ordinary 6 or 12 volt batteries installed into Motor Cars, Boats & Aeroplanes alike".*

Dennis Noble had already started to build a new career in radio technology. A thought crossed my mind during the research, what if he had survived the war & managed to continue with his research, just where would his career have progressed? Possibly employment working with military or civilian communications!

Annie Evans remembers Dennis becoming engaged to a young local girl whose identity is still a mystery. She apparently resided in London. Annie recalls" *I only met her once on a visit she made to Retford, her photograph indicates a pretty young brunette with a warm smile ("this she surely had").*

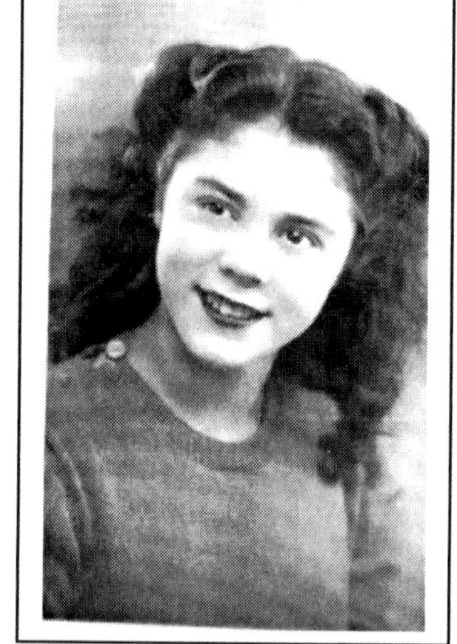

"Is This Polly Patchy Pocket Dennis's Fiancée

Could this have been the young girl seen accompanying Dennis on his visits to the cinema at Chichester. Were they young lovers? Could she have been the elusive "Polly Patchy Pocket" a nickname given to the young girl often seen accompanying Dennis? Maybe it would account for the 1/6 penny Cinema ticket discovered still in his wallet after fifty-six years, buried with him.

Dennis Noble that shy young man with abilities to attract the best qualities from everyone, a young lad who could have belonged to any mother in the country & sent to fight a war, soon to be immortalised for ever as

One of the Few'

Annie Evans concludes her tribute

"Dennis came to our home on a short visit two weeks before he died, I shall always remember him as he was with pride".

John Noble
Dennis's Brother

Annie Noble
Dennis's Mother

Harry Noble
(Kneeling Bottom Left)

Top... Hallcroft Road Retford where the Noble Family lived.

Bottom .The Baptist church where Dennis frequently attended.

PATENT SPECIFICATION

533,373

Application Date: Aug 15, 1939. No. 23534/39.

Complete Specification Left: Aug. 15, 1940.

Complete Specification Accepted: Feb. 12, 1941.

PROVISIONAL SPECIFICATION

Means for Operating Electric Shaving Apparatus

We, MASTERADIO LIMITED, a British Company, and DENIS NOBLE, a British Subject, both of 1, Newton Street, High Holborn, London, W.C.2, do hereby declare the nature of this invention to be as follows:—

Electric razors or shaving devices of the "mains" type, that is, those which require a voltage of 50 to 260 volts to operate them, have the disadvantage that they can only be used where there is a source of electricity of the necessary voltage available.

This invention has for its object to provide a device which will enable such razors to be used where only a small voltage is obtainable and has for its chief object to provide means whereby such razors can be operated from the ordinary 6 or 12 volt batteries installed in motor cars, motor boats, aeroplanes and like vehicles, but it is equally applicable for use with private electric systems which are usually of low voltage or from any low voltage electric battery.

In one convenient manner of carrying the invention into effect, we provide as a separate unit, a suitable transformer, giving the required output voltage and having a vibrator in its primary circuit. When required for use, the transformer is connected through its primary circuit to an accumulator or other low voltage supply and the razor is connected to the secondary circuit having the necessary voltage. If the razor is adapted to operate on direct current, suitable means for rectifying the current would be provided.

The unit may be attached in a suitable position on the vehicle if desired but it would preferably be of a portable nature and connected up when required by suitable leads, so that it could be used in any vehicle or position.

Instead of the device being in the form of a separate unit, it could be incorporated with the razor in a single housing.

The unit may also be attached by means of a plug and socket to an existing radio receiver, the said receiver being operated from a low voltage D.C source (or another convenient means). The above obviates the use of a separate unit if a radio receiver with suitable sockets is available.

The transformer unit could be adapted to fixed predetermined input and output voltages or could be constructed so as to be suitable for 6 or 12 volt input for use on vehicles or 32 to 50 volt input for use on private lighting systems and a 100 to 260 volt output to enable any make or voltage of razor to be operated.

It will be seen that the device is particularly suitable in enabling tourists, campers and those temporarily staying in places where there is no ordinary source of electricity to use their own electric razors.

Dated this 15th day of August, 1939.
WITHERS & SPOONER,
Chartered Patent Agents,
148—150, Holborn, London, E.C.1,
Agents for the Applicants.

COMPLETE SPECIFICATION

Means for Operating Electric Shaving Apparatus

We, MASTERADIO LIMITED, a British Company, and DENIS NOBLE, a British Subject, both formerly of 1, Newton Street, High Holborn, London, W.C.2, now of Vibrant Works, 193, Rickmansworth Road, Watford, in the County of Herts, do hereby declare the nature of this invention and in what manner the same is to be performed, to be particularly described and ascertained in and by the following statement:—

This invention relates to means for operating electric shaving apparatus.

Electric razors or shaving devices of the "mains" type, that is, those which require a voltage of 50 to 260 volts to operate them, have the disadvantage that they can only be used where there is a

[*Price* 1/-]

British Patent 533,373

Specification for an Electric Shaver invented by Dennis Noble on behalf of Master Radio Ltd.

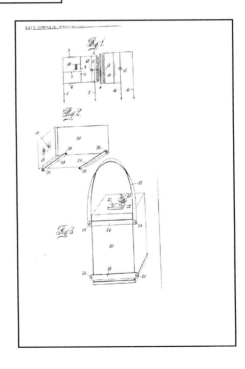

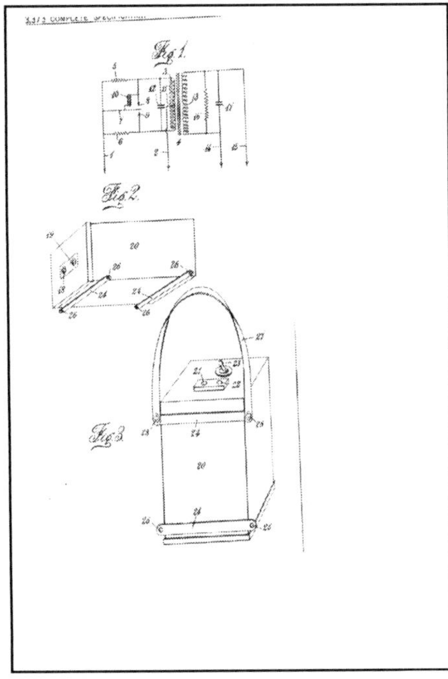

Drawing of Circuit unit, needed when operating an Electric Razor from One's car, or other low voltage supply i.e., Boat or Aeroplane

Retford Town War Memorial

LEAVES OF A LOG BOOK.

Dennis Noble enlisted as a pilot under training (AC.2. U/T) in the Royal Air force Volunteer Reserves 8th October 1938. At 5ft 9ins, with brown eyes & dark brown hair, aged 18 years, Dennis was about to take the Flying Instruction fundamental to fulfil his dream. Before he could commence, he was promoted to Sergeant on the 9th October 1938, the minimum rank to be held for pilot status.

Redhill Aerodrome in Surrey, close to the London to Brighton railway line & near to Gatwick station, is an airfield very much in the forefront of aviation, still training pilots but now for the CAA, Private Pilots licence in both fixed wing & Helicopter syllabus, this was to be his first training airfield & one close to his heart.

Sgt DENNIS NOBLE. 9th October 1938.

On his arrival, he would observe a parked **De Havilland DH 60 Moth** an aeroplane that would play a very important part in his training. The day had arrived for him to take his first flight. His instructor talked him through the pre flight checks, before continuing into the phases of flight. "Something I myself experienced many years later while about to venture into the unknown aspirations of flight an experience one never forgets"*(Author).*

Adrenaline pumping & one's nerves well on edge, you acclimatise yourself to the experiences that lay ahead. Dennis's Log Book records his first flight on 9th October 1938 the very next day after joining the flying school being duration of 33 minutes. During the next two years, he flew many different types from the slow biplanes to the fast RAF fighters of the period.
We will tackle the logistics of the aeroplanes he flew in a later chapter. For his first flight to be achieved the formidable pre flight checks both visual & Mechanical must be carried out, checking the appearance of the aeroplane & possible obstructions nearby. Checking for torn Canvas, or damage to the wheels & tyres. Then inside of the cockpit fundamentals such as the control column & rudder pedal for free movement, also accuracy of the instruments a set pattern is laid out for one to follow every time flight is undertaken. Magneto switches 'on' then the mechanic swings the propeller & its 60hp Cirrus engine fires into action, a check of the gauges indicates oil pressures 'Ok'.
Wind from the propeller creates a slipstream momentarily blowing small particles of grass & moister into one's face.
The instructor gives the thumbs up sign, indicating that its time to taxi, as the engine revs increase one feels the vibration & bumps as the aeroplane moves slowly forwards, air speed increasing with the grass rushing past at an alarming rate then gently the aeroplane lifts into the air, a moment of calmness surrounds you are gaining height. Suddenly, you look out from the cockpit, trees are noticeably getting smaller. Smoke from nearby chimneys indicating wind direction.
Ones stomach churns, as the motion of flight resembles a fairground carousel. It's easy to be come disorientated especially when in a steep dive or turn, as the earth takes on a new dimsion before one's eyes, soon these feelings will become an everyday occurrence & one soon adjusted to flying. Although only a short flight Dennis would have felt the agility of the DH 60 throughout the manoeuvres his instructor carried out. Now it was time to land.

As the engine cuts to idle speed a slight popping from the exhaust gave would have given cause for concern, this was normal, nevertheless gave him a fright, as it was his first experience. The nose of the aeroplane steadily pointed towards the grass field bought the ground rushing towards him. Then suddenly a slight amount of wind shear perhaps 5-8 knots whisked from behind a hanger moving the aircraft from its flight path he watched as the control column move from side to side as the instructor gained control from this sudden gust. Gently pulling back on the stick as the wheels touched soil again, the boundary fence at first rushing past then slowly decreasing as they came to a halt. Finally the engine was cut & a feeling of accomplishment with perhaps a sigh of relief as silence prevailed.

At least now Dennis knew the standards he must achieve, there was a great deal to learn if he was to fulfil his dream to become a fighter pilot in the RAF. As a member of the Royal Air Force Volunteer Reserve, he became known as a weekend flyer, because many fellow students maintained normal weekday professions & like Dennis travelled to the Airfield at weekends.

During the evenings, he studied the RAF Air publications learning them from beginning to end. For example, he must learn the petrol, oil & ignition circuits of the Moth, also the art of propeller swinging. Something one learns with the utmost caution as a good foothold on the ground is vital, there are no second chances if you slip pulling the prop through its cycle, ' all propellers must be treated as live as any slight movement can cause an engine to fire into action, with 'disastrous results'. This procedure would have been laid down in the FTM *(Fight training manual part 1 chp 11, par24).* Dennis would have studied this text before his next flight. Although the RAF would have paid for his training, the cost would have been around £2 per hour at Redhill Flying Club if paying for training oneself. Today's fees would be in the region of £140 per hour. Dennis flew the DH 60 Moth only twice more on 22 & 23 October 1938, studying the effects of the controls in flight

During these initial flights, he would be able to hold the controls loosely while the instructor advised him of the correct technique, teaching his student to use only light pressure on the controls & not to tug at the stick causing sudden unnecessary movements. Dennis's instructor was **Flt Lt Evans,** giving guidance to yet another pupil placed under his comforting wing. Sitting in the front seat Of the DH 60 his scarf thrashing in the wind, nevertheless a reassuring face if problems arose. On his return, from his third flight, Dennis was allowed to taxi the aircraft back to the parking area. Gentle control was needed on the ground owing to the fact that forward visibility is restricted by the high attitude of the engine. The Moth is a Tail dragger & fitted with a rear skid instead of a wheel therefore the utmost care had to be taken when turning on the ground, one must remember not to turn too sharply as the tail of the aeroplane comes around quickly & may cause damage to other parked aeroplanes, or ground personnel in the vicinity.

De HAVILLAND DH 60 MOTH

By his third lesson, Dennis had flown three different DH60 Moths, 'adding them to his flying Log Book'. Although a beautiful aircraft Dennis longed for the chance to fly mono wing planes, this became reality on 5th November 1938 in the shape of the **Miles Magister M14a**. A wonderful touring aeroplane of the 1930s powered by the 130hp Rolls-Royce Gipsy Major engine an aircraft with many flying trophies awarded to the type. Such as a flight from England to Australia, while completing in the Mac Robinson Trophy race from Mildenhall, Suffolk, to Melbourne Australia 1934, it also proved to be an ideal training aeroplane.
"Excitement would be the one word summing up his feelings, when he reported to **Flt Lt Dale** his first instructor who was to show him the layout of the Miles Magister". A splendour compared to the Cockpit layout of the Moth, one could see clearly displayed gauges, the Compass, Altimeter, Turn co-ordinator, Rev counter even a cockpit lamp, it seems very basic but to him it was Technology at it's best. Dennis soon clocked up 56 hours on the type, his logbook recalls that on the 23 April 1939, he practised Spin & Recovery attitudes with instructor **Flt, Lt Coleman** in the front seat taking control & demonstrating the manoeuvres. Disorientation makes this manoeuvre dangerous because of the increasing revolutions of the aircraft during the spin. Air speed must be checked early or the spin can become 'fatal'.
To recover from this situation one must first determine direction of rotation, close the throttle stick in neutral position, rudder pedal in opposite direction to spin, "wait" then slowly pull out of ensuing dive, levelling off & increasing power, then back into normal climb attitude, "easy when you now how but when learning is an experience one never forgets" Dennis made many other flights similar to this one building towards that precious moment 'ones first solo flight' entered in his Log book as 17th May 1939 flying **N3892** A most cherished moment for all pilots as it brings one into the realms of professionalism, an achievement that makes one exuberant. No other flight would be the same as this one in the faithful old Maggie.

There is very much more to learn before one gains control of a Hurricane. "No other flight would be the same as this one in the faithful old Maggie". Purely by chance this flight was made in the first Magister he had flown **N3742.** May 26 1939 provided an opportune time with the weather on his side he spent 45 minutes airborne with **Flying Officer Lash** practicing his low flying skills, watching the speed of trees zooming past makes it quite awesome. Dennis had managed to put up an average response to his tuition so-far with his instructors putting him forward for his first flying test. Under the watchful eye of **Flying Officer Adams,** he took his Navigation test 29th May 1939, using the three-point flight plans from Redhill to Hamble in Hampshire returning to Redhill. "Observing breath-taking views along the way, from 5000ft one could see some 30 miles." Southampton water was visual with the Estuary to the river Hamble to the North & the aerodrome situated on the West Bank.
"Hitler's aggression during June 1939 was increasingly causing concern, & it seemed that the government would have to take drastic steps". The need for pilots was increasing, therefore Dennis's training had to be rushed ahead as his Country might call on his services at anytime. 17-18 June 1939 he recorded 4hrs 20mins flying time, his hours were stepped up with his full time job in London was now taking second place. On 2nd July, he took off from Redhill with instructor **Flt Lt Lovell Gauge.** His job was to assess Dennis's flying skills. Triumphantly he passed as a fully-fledged pilot. Nevertheless, he still had a long way to go, because this was only the first part of the course. Dennis now had to satisfy the RAF he had the capabilities to become an RAF fighter pilot. Flying manoeuvres such as formation flying, & battle training this time flying more powerful aeroplanes such as the **Hawker Audax** slightly favouring the Hawker Hart in power, but both fitted with the Roll-Royce Kestrel engine. The Audax could reach speeds in excess of 170mph but was much faster in the climb.

On the 13th August 1939, Flying instructor **Flt Lt Barrett** gave Dennis his first chance to fly Hawker Audax K2001. He would have noticed the rather large undercarriage wheels as he stepped into the cockpit, a trimming tab that moved over the whole length of the tail plane, Also different to him would have been the Radiator Flap allowing the pilot to control the heat range of the engine by opening or shutting the cowling flap.

Dennis would soon be flying many different aircraft types, each with it's own characteristics & something new-fangled every time, therefore reading the pilots notes to each aircraft type was an important task during the evenings.

HAWKER AUDAX

" Peacetime flying was running out fast" an entry in Dennis's Logbook, underlined states "**Declaration of War" 3-9-39.** His last peacetime flight was 27 August 1939 practicing exercise 15 steep turns & exercise16 forced landings in Hart (T) K6805 & was subsequently passed out from No 15 E & R FTS Redhill by chief instructor Flt Dale, with an assessment grading, stamped in his logbook as Average ability.

An initial period learning RAF foot Drill or perhaps better known

As square bashing! Dennis arrived at No 1 LT training wing Cambridgeshire 2 September 1939, although something of a break from flying it was also a requirement for everyone with a service career to participate. As a pilot he would shortly be called upon to defend the shores of Britain from the Luftwaffe therefore drill requirements were minimal. RAF training is probably the most stringent in the world, & perfection was of great importance for young pilots passing through the various training stages, it could even help save lives when suddenly faced with the misfortune of battle against an already hardened enemy, who had gained experience fighting during the Spanish civil war, & were still learning the art of warfare by attacking Poland. German pilots & crews were very highly trained with formidable experience. This made them excellent marksmen; many young British pilots fell to the guns of the German bomber crews. RAF pilots learned quickly if they were to survive against a well-equipped enemy. After a short leave he reported to 11 Flying training unit at Shawbury, on 31st January 1940 for advanced training. After a spell learning basic RAF drill, it became necessary to reacquaint him with flight procedure. His instructor, **Warrant Officer Ashdown** set out a refresher course, but due to bad weather he could not start until 18th February 1940, the winter of 39-40 was exceptional, with heavy snow & severe frost. Eventually he undertook the task set by his instructors thereby re-establishing his flying abilities. After which he was awarded with a four-day pass. A welcome break gave him a chance to see his family & visit his brother John in London before returning to Shawbury 5th March 1940. 'Flying **Hawker Hart K5021 on** April Fools Day what a day & to start his 15 hr test, concentrating on the aspects flying skills, luck prevailed & a pass rate of average was achieved. 'Although more flights were carried out during the days ahead, there was never time to look back, so intensive was the training that he wrote home to his sister Phyllis complaining of tiredness.

The strain was beginning to show & sleepless nights would soon be confronting him as the war drew closer to home.

Flying continued 13th April 1940 in **Hart 6539** with Dennis at the controls & **Flt Dunworth** as his instructor & Dennis's first night exercise, something he did not have to endure very frequently.

May 1940 arrived & pilots were urgently needed, & basic skills had to make way for the chores of aggressive flying & 'how to destroy one's enemy'. A Variety of aircraft attached to the unit were soon recorded in his Logbook, two more **Harts K4982** & **Audax K7407**. Completing various exercises such as spinning & aerobatic manoeuvres trying to eradicate attacking enemy planes. These courses soon came to an end when **Squadron Leader J.D.A. McBratney** decided that it was time to move on, sending him to No 6 O. T.U. Sutton Bridge Lincolnshire, for final duties before being sent to the front line where he was desperately required, with his flying time now totalling 186 hours 20 minutes, & 4hours 50 minutes in the Link trainer. "A very early type of flight simulator, basic but nevertheless a practical source used for teaching pilots the principles of flight, including instrument flying. A very useful device as it could be used during bad weather for practice flying indoors. Dennis was soon faced with the prospect of flying the fast monoplanes, such as the North American Harvard or Texan, as it was known in America. To make sure that his capabilities met the requirements laid down in the flying manuals Dennis studied each journal with the utmost care. Up to now the only monoplane he had flown was the Miles Magister, & compared to the Harvard powered by the Pratt & Whitney Radial R1340 Wasp engine, the Magister was no match. The Harvard was designed as a USAAF trainer, ideal to learn battle manoeuvres & air to air combat. This is a very noisy aeroplane with its own unique sound, with the engine set at 2200 Rpm its propeller tips travelled at just below supersonic, creating a beating noise that still turns the heads of crowds at air shows all over the world. 8th July 1940, Dennis took off in **Harvard 7176** under the watchful eye of **P/O Lewis**. A new experience for Dennis was the retractable undercarriage & unlike the fixed landing gear, he now had to remember to lower the wheels.

An operation many pilots even by today's standards have forgotten causing embarrassment as the aircraft makes its final approach. Sometimes the go-around procedure is implemented just as the pilot remembers Ah, pausing for a second before increasing power & making another attempt.

Satisfying his tutors Dennis was given the unexpected task of flying **Hurricane L1548.** Walking towards his machine must have been a remarkable occasion. With the knowledge he had gained over the past year, he climbed into the cockpit. L1548 was the first Hurricane to enter 111 Squadron at Northolt 15th September 1937 & eventually transferred to 11 O.T.U. After his initial checks, he opened the throttle, & applied full rudder correcting the airflow blowing backwards underneath & revolving around the fuselage onto the tail causing the aircraft to yaw. Gathering speed across the grass the tail lifting into the air, presenting the pilot with a better forward vision, slowly pulling back on the control column the Hurricane lifts into the air, gathering speed for the climb to 5000 feet, into the vast open space of the heavens. Dennis would have been full of delight with his accomplishment flying this marvellous warbird. Upon landing he climbed out & was met with the smell of the hot Merlin engine, its aroma unrelenting in the air along with the exhaust crackling as it cools.

During his stay at Sutton Bridge he flew 11 Hurricanes on 30 occasions along with various other aircraft types such as the **Miles Master** & **Fairey Battle,** making one such flight with **P/O Forrester** observing practice air attacks. The Battle was similar to the Hurricane but was vastly over weight & slow even though the Rolls-Royce Merlin powered it. Dennis finally finished his training 30 July 1940, unbeknown to him was the fact that he would only survive another Month achieving the status of----

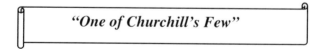

"One of Churchill's Few"

Year 1939. Month	Date	Aircraft Type	Aircraft No.	Pilot, or 1st Pilot	2nd Pilot, Pupil or Passenger	Duty (Including Results and Remarks).
—	—	—	—	—	—	Totals Brought Forward
MAY.	17.	MAGISTER	N3792.	SELF	SOLO.	FIRST SOLO.
MAY.	17.	MAGISTER	N3842	FLT WALTER	SELF	7. TAKING OFF INTO WIND. 8. APPROACHES AND LANDINGS.
MAY	17.	MAGISTER	N3842.	SELF	SOLO.	7. TAKING OFF INTO WIND. 8. APPROACHES AND LANDINGS.
MAY	17.	MAGISTER	N3842.	SELF	SOLO	7. TAKING OFF INTO WIND. 8. APPROACHES AND LANDINGS.
MAY	18.	MAGISTER	L8336	SELF	SOLO.	6. MEDIUM TURNS. 7. TAKING OFF INTO WIND. 8. APPROACHES AND LANDINGS.
MAY	18.	MAGISTER	N3805	SELF	SOLO.	6. MEDIUM TURNS. 7. TAKING OFF INTO WIND. 8. APPROACHES AND LANDINGS.
MAY	19.	MAGISTER.	N3836.	F/O ADAMS.	SELF.	12. SIDESLIPPING.
MAY	19	MAGISTER	N3792	SELF	SOLO.	6. MEDIUM TURNS.
MAY	20	MAGISTER	N3812	SELF	SOLO.	6. MEDIUM TURNS.

GRAND TOTAL [Cols. (1) to (10)] 16 Hrs. 00 Mins.

Totals Carried Forward

Page from Sgt Nobles Logbook.

First Solo Flight

This scroll commemorates

Sergeant D. Noble
Royal Air Force

held in honour as one who served King and Country in the world war of 1939-1945 and gave his life to save mankind from tyranny. May his sacrifice help to bring the peace and freedom for which he died.

A STORM IS BREWING.

After three days leave, Dennis was ordered to report to 43 squadron based at Tangmere, West Sussex. A front line airfield with the South Downs standing to the North & Chichester three miles to the West, the A27 Brighton to Portsmouth road running East to West of the aerodrome boundary. Already in the thick of the fighting defending shipping convoys in the Channel. Also fending off German raiders crossing the coast to attack Fighter Commands Airfields attacks that were increasing considerably. Dennis reported to Tangmere on 3rd August 1940 together with fellow sergeants **A.L.M. Deller, H.F. Montgomery & P/O C.K. Gray,** all completing their training at 6 O.T.U. then thrown in at the deep end to gain battle experience. Two of them were fated to die during the coming weeks, with two surviving the German onslaught. Fortunately, they had arrived on a quiet day with very little air activity, giving them precious time to familiarise themselves with the Aerodrome & meet some of the other pilots in their assigned flight. Let us join them on their trek around Tangmere Aerodrome taking in some of the surroundings that were to be "home from home". 19th November 1916 set the place for this famous airfield when Geoffrey Dorman R.F.C made a forced landing in a field at Bayley's farm Tangmere, while returning from Shoreham to Gosport in a **FE26.** Comprising of approximately 200 acres it was not long before the prospects of such a large area made it an ideal site to develop an airfield. 'They noticed three service hangers & a 300 foot shed built at the end of the World War One, to house Handley Page bombers' the new brick accommodation barracks & workshops. 'The Fire station' & operations building, not forgetting the ground crews hurriedly going about their chores, squadron Hurricanes parked at dispersal locations with pilots waiting for the telephone to ring with that famous war cry 'Scramble Scramble' soon to be reality for the four young men fresh from training school & eager to take on the best of the Luftwaffe. Sunday 4th & Monday 5th August also proved to be quiet giving Dennis time to settle in with B flight.

Tuesday 6th August 1940, the weather report for the day was low cloud; therefore, the Luftwaffe would most likely reduce air activity to reconnaissance patrols. Although now operational, Dennis spent 1hour 20 minutes practicing formation flying, practice attacks, & fast battle climbs to 25000 feet. He also made his first operational flight with 43 Squadron carrying out a sector reconnaissance sortie. His flights during the day were made in **Hurricane L1739 FT-Q** & one of the first Hurricanes issued to 43 Squadron 0n 15 December 1938. L1739 was destroyed eight days later, along with **Sgt H F Montgomery** who had joined 43 squadron on the same day as Dennis Noble. This tragic loss brought home the realities of war & the necessity to learn that death really was just around the corner, a time to take note of the advice that the more experience pilots had to offer. Having spent only 25 hours on Hurricanes did not make Dennis an experienced fighter pilot compared to other members of the squadron such as **Sgt Hallowes, F/O Frank Carey, & Sqdn Ldr Badger** already credited with destroying enemy aircraft. Dennis also flew **L1736 FT-H on** the 6th August, which had a history of destroying a Me Bf 109, also damage to an Me110 on the 1 June 1940 with **F/O Edmonds** at the controls during the Dunkirk evacuation. Alas this aircraft was to meet it's fate on 16th August 1940 when its Merlin engine burst into flames after a coolant leak, with the pilot **Sgt Crisp** breaking a collarbone while baling out.

L to R. Sgt Mills, P/O Gray, F/O Woods-Scawen Sgt Montgomery, Sgt Deller, Flt Dickie Reynell

Sgt Dennis Noble is Standing in door way

43 squadron pilots 'B' Flight August 1940. Left to Right... P/O Roy Du Vivier (Kneeling) Sgt Noble. F/O Upton. Squadron Leader J.V.C Badger (Seated). P/O Gorrie. P/O Van den Hove. Sgt Hallowes. Four of these pilots flewHurricane P3179 in action

FIGHTER SQUADRON
43
43
ROYAL AIR FORCE
GLORIA FINIS

Tangmere's newly appointed Pilots had to learn instantly the navigational landmarks surrounding the aerodrome. Most of this experience was gained during non-operational flights, but they would have had to make the most of every flight as an emergency could prevail. The shortest route home would be extremely fundamental to ones safe return. Dennis would need to observe landmarks such as the unmistakable shape of the Isle of Wight & the silver sheen of the Solent. Selsey Bill is a point in the coast that assisted many pilots home, not forgetting the tall spire of Chichester Cathedral & Halnaker Windmill the oldest tower mill in Sussex, built 1740. Two piers extending out to sea distinguished Brighton & Worthing to the East of the aerodrome. Also the coast railway line travelling East to West. An abundance of airfields were also located along the coast such as Shoreham, & Fleet Air arm establishment at Ford. Westhampnett only two miles North West of Tangmere, & still an active airfield now better known as Goodwood once home to 145 Squadron Hurricanes & 602 Squadron Spitfires. Further west were Hamble Nr Southampton & Thorney Island. A Hurricane could travel an extensive area in 30 minutes & would have given Dennis a good knowledge of the surrounding area. He would have noticed barrage balloons situated around the harbour at Southampton, but would most definitely have bypassed the Ack Ack Batteries along the coast just in case a trigger-happy gunner decided to shoot first before checking the identity of the aircraft overhead.
6th August 1940, Dennis was ordered to practice fast battle climbs to 25000ft, & to make a 30-minute reconnaissance of the sector. With the sour taste of oxygen & the cold biting its way through his flying suit he could not wait to return to base & a hot cup of tea. With the exception of a couple of thunderstorms, 7th August 1940 was not a bad day. Dennis was soon airborne flying Hurricane **L1836** this time practicing cloud flying & Dog fighting as practice makes perfect & can save lives. Even in war, these flights were designed to teach young pilots being sent to the front line, that they may have to fly in bad weather conditions such as Cumulus cloud

associated with stormy weather. Thermals making a bumpy ride as rising hot air & down draughts from the cold air pitch the aeroplane around; with no horizon to align to therefore one must rely on the indications given by the artificial Horizon & the Turn & Slip indicator. Keeping straight & level with changing airspeed in these conditions brings out the best in ones flying abilities & is physically demanding. The hurricane did not have the luxury of radar as today's fighters have just a hope & a prayer that no one else is flying in your airspace. Dennis must have found this extremely hard as his ability at instrument flying were noted in his logbook by his instructor at O.T.U as below average, definitely a weak mark for blind flying. We must consider though that he had only 12 hours duel instruction in cloud & 5 hours as pilot in command, over the previous two years, & in much slower aircraft. L1836 had been damaged earlier in the year when 43 squadron were stationed in Wick, Scotland & was out of commission until June 1940, only to be grounded once again 4 September 1940 when Belgian ace **P/O Albert van den hove,** after destroying a Me 110, received a hit in the glycol tank, with the engine overheated he made a emergency landing at Ford aerodrome. Thursday 8th 9th & 10th August bought a welcome rest without enemy action affecting Dennis & no entry was placed in his logbook. That didn't mean though that the days passed without cause for alarm as a convoy of twenty ships needed protection, 43 squadron were scrambled & 12 Hurricanes took off to fulfil their orders. **F/O Frank Carey** of A flight described this action. An array of enemy aircraft had formed up consisting of Stukas, Me110s & Me 109s. Frank Carey recalls "I climbed with my section to engage the 109s leaving the lower section to tackle the bombers, in the fight that followed I lost contact with my other two aircraft, when I spotted 109s in formation which I took at first to be Hurricanes & went off to join them. On discovering my mistake I was happy to note that they had not seen me, I continued until I got behind one of the outside members of the formation. I had just settled down to fire at this aircraft with some success as bits started

To fly off it, when suddenly a large explosion nearly blew me upside down, an Me 110 saw what I had done & was sitting about 30 yards behinds me with its 20mm shells blowing up my port wing magazine, leaving a hole large enough for a man to crawl through. By the time I had righted the aeroplane all the 109s had disappeared & with no sign of the Me 110, I laboriously climbed to get over the convoy again, when I was jumped by some 110s. This time they blew off one elevator & damaged the rudder. Before I could gain my senses I realised that I had been hit in the arm, so I thought discretion was the better part of valour & slowly brought the remains back to base".
Meanwhile another Hurricane **P3179** arrived at Tangmere to help fill the gaps increasingly becoming wider, as there were more pilots than planes, something that changed rather quickly as the day's ahead wore on. Hurricane P3179 had been built at Brockworth by the Gloster Aircraft Company 16 February 1940 & was stored waiting for conversion to the three bladed Rotol Propeller. P3179 was to be the most frequent machine allocated to Dennis Noble also the aircraft that was to be his tomb for fifty-six years. **Sgt H.J.L. Hallowes** downed a Me 109 during the same engagement over the channel its pilot baling out from the stricken machine as it weaved its way towards the sea with flames & black Cordite smoke trailing behind. 43 squadron suffered the loss of two pilots **P/O J. Cruttenden** flying Hurricane **P3781** crashing 10 miles South of the Isle of Wight at 16.45 hrs. **P/O Oelofse** was killed in Hurricane **P3468** he is buried in St Andrews Churchyard Tangmere. **P/O C.A. Woods-Scrawen** managed to land his damaged Hurricane **P3214** safely at Tangmere after combat in the same battle in which he suffered a knee injury. Another stricken aircraft **P3267** flown by **P/O, O H.C. Upton** made a forced landing at Ford aerodrome, its engine had seized after the loss of coolant. Friday 9th August 1940, brought yet another day of little air activity & a state of readiness remained all day, & without any respite for aircrews remaining at dispersals. Saturday 10th August, bad weather continued, keeping the Luftwaffe at bay.

Well apart from a few nuisance raids, that kept the RAF on their toes'. Excessive rainfall had saturated Tangmere airfield & movements were restricted to the apron area unless extremely necessary. Sunday 11th August 1940 A few raids over Kent started early in the morning with Lympne aerodrome being bombed at 08.16 hrs, with hit & run raids throughout the day.

Dennis currently on readiness with B flight was allocated Hurricane **V7221** a fairly new machine in which he was scrambled three times throughout the day, 'these became known as X Plots throughout the squadron.' These raids did not materialise into anything much, but nevertheless gave Dennis another 1 hour 40 minutes battle flying experience.

Monday 12th August 1940 bought increased activity along the coast, Hitler had decided the time was right for the destruction of the RAF airfields, but first he must eliminate the early defence warning system that England had installed at strategic points along the coast from Dover to Ventnor on the Isle of Wight. Germany was not fully advised of the advancement of the Home chain Radar, or even if it was fully operational, Germany could ill afford to take the chance. The Luftwaffe was immediately ordered to knock out the masts. Dunkirk between Canterbury & Faversham Kent was one such station, with four wooden at 340 ft & four metal pylons at 365feet & three large platforms linked with a steel ladder between each. These pylons were visible for miles, not something one could camouflage. Also they made exceptional navigation landmarks on the unblemished landscape. 'Standing at the top of Boughton Hill in the small village of Dunkirk' local people were about to suffer a taste of war. When at 18.12hrs just as local residents were finished their evening tea, Luftwaffe Stukas paid a surprise visit dropping 250 & 500kg bombs luckily without causing damage to the pylons, although superficial damage was caused by bombs to out buildings with a few craters scattered around the station & surrounding woodland. Regrettably there were two casualties one a civilian with serious injuries; both were taken to Canterbury hospital.

Damage was sustained to under ground cables although it seemed to be significant, it only took a few hours to repair bringing it back to operational standards. Nineteen years later in January 1959," the people of Dunkirk were to suffer once again the disruption of what seemed like a re-enactment of the German attack of 1940. The Ministry of Defence decided that due to the advancement of Radar there was no need for the pylons to remain. Demolition crews set charges beneath two supporting legs of each pylon, with the idea that when the charges exploded these tall structures would slowly fall in the direction required as the two remaining feet would act as hinges. "As a small boy I remember watching them fall gracefully to the ground, with a slow defined dignity, something the Germans never achieved". All was not lost as one of these fine works of art still stands proud & still used for communications, although reduced in height, much of the home chain station is still visible although covered in undergrowth as nature has taken control. The concrete support pillars & the bomb proof Ops room are still in remarkable condition standing with dignity as a tribute to those that served there during War & Peacetime.

DUNKIRK RADAR STATION
Operations Room taken during 1999

Tuesday 13 August 1940, France was suffering from poor weather with Luftwaffe airfields at Luftlotten fog bound. By late morning attacks on RAF airfields were imminent, & Dennis was once again in action this time however he suffered a few problems when his Hurricane **V7221** suffered hits fired from the rear gunner of a Junkers Ju 88 bomber in Dennis's own words "received bullet in Radiator, retired from fight with glycol leak, forced landed at Ford ". Dennis managed to obtain a lift back to Tangmere just in time to be Scrambled once again this time in **L1836** at 16.00 hrs, a sentence from one of his letters to his sister sums up how he felt, "Time does not stop & leaves no time for rest Your loving brother Dennis". Suffering from tiredness the stresses of battle began to take hold & his ability to respond quickly to sudden distractions must have made it difficult when flying, therefore bringing a lower rate of survival. Wednesday 14th August, the Luftwaffe put on a stream of heavy raids attacking the usual targets. One such raid bought B flight into action when patrolling the Isle of Wight, they spotted a lone Ju 88 & immediately gave chase after giving a short burst each, 'the rear gunner fell silent' & the starboard engine burst into flames, the aircraft then fell into a steep dive no parachutes were seen indicating that the crew had perished, it then crashed into the sea off the Needles. As part of a team Dennis had contributed & entered it into his logbook, he was flying Hurricane **V7366**. It was a busy day for 43 squadron as they were scrambled once again 15 minutes after landing. Unfortunately, the day did not end with out loss as **Sgt Montgomery** perished in his Hurricane just off Beachy Head, the first of the four young flyers that joined the squadron together on the 3rd August to be killed. 'A lost friend' this must have been an enormous blow to Dennis certainly bought the aspect of death closer. Thursday 15th August, began peacefully for 43 squadron, despite a beautiful day, this was because the Germans were once again fog bound. It was almost mid morning before a strike force of 60 Stukas with fighter escorts of 40 Me 109s attacked Manston Lympne & Hawkinge. By mid afternoon the raids increased with 90 Dorniers & 130 fighters

These were the total Dornier Gruppen Loftflotte with bases at Antwerp-Seurne & St Trond in Belgium, this raid was by far the largest seen over Kent. Giving the people of the towns & villages cause for concern, wondering just what the future had in store. It was now time to take precautions such as erecting the newly arrived Anderson shelter into the back yard of homes, designed to give protection from flying glass & other missiles. The town's folk of Dover & Folkstone had already been suffering from shells fired across the channel by Germanys railway guns positioned in occupied France. This part of Kent became known as 'Hell Fire Corner'.

43 squadron were in the air once again late afternoon intercepting bombers crossing the coast, suffering damage to Hurricane **P3971** after a hit in the glycol tank by return fire from a bomber from 4/LG1 **Squadron leader J.V.C (tubby) Badger** was unhurt. The second misfortune was Hurricane **R4107 FT-B** with bullet strikes to the main spar of the wing but repairable **P/O C.A Woods-Scawen** was also unhurt. During the last few days Hurricane **P3179** was bought into action, passing as operational by **Flt Morgan** after Test flying it for it's A&E Certificate. P3179 took to the air with **P/O Roy Du Vivier** at 10.35 on the 12 August & signed out next day to **P/O Van den hove** at 14.15 to 1500 hrs. On the 15th August, P/O Du Vivier took control of P3179 flying two X Plots, Dennis had been allocated **V7336** & while on patrol he chased a Junkers Ju 88, he remarked in his logbook "Fired all ammunition at Ju 88 but without apparent effect". Landing back at base tired & weary he was ordered back into the air to practice night flying in the Tangmere circuit at 21.15 to 22.10hrs, flying **L1836** I do not suppose Dennis was very much in favour of this flight but it was necessary to gain confidence & experience, sleep would come later. Friday 16th August 1940, recorded history shows commitment & courageous acts of Heroism throughout time with warriors devoting their sincerity towards a cause they believed to be right. No one could be more devoted than the pilots & ground crews of 43 squadron

It was really just the matter of time before Britain fell to its knees, materials were becoming difficult to locate as Convoys came under severe attacks & vital cargos were destroyed. The RAF was trying to put up fighters to repel the waves of Luftwaffe Bombers intensifying by the day. Tiredness was contributing towards the increasing number of casualties, but although in need of rest & short of pilots Britain had to push those capable of defending our shores to the limits & sometimes beyond one's hidden capability. The 16th August was a day of intensive action when Stuka dive-bombers at 13.00hrs devastated Tangmere Aerodrome. Deploying direct hits on the sick quarters, officer's mess, & two Hangers. Also various parked aircraft, six Blenheim's, seven Hurricanes, & one Miles Magister, but the aerodrome was never declared non-operational. Dennis played his part in the attack, flying with blue section as blue four. Whilst engaging the enemy at 12,000ft he made his only confirmed 'Kill'. In his own words he tells the story of this action quoted from his combat report; "I *was flying number four position in blue section when we attacked a formation of Ju87s, selecting* a *machine* I *closed the range & commenced to fire at 300yrds*, I *gave* a *short burst, the rear gunner ceased to return fire. After* a *second burst at 200yrds, the bomb dropped from the machine also another black object. Smoke was issuing from the engine cowling, the machine then did* a *diving turn* to *the left. I followed giving two deflection burst at 100yrds, it then dived towards the sea flattening out for two or three seconds before crashing approximately One mile south east of Selsey Bill.* I *then climbed to attack another enemy machine, after a short burst at three to four hundred yards my ammunition was expended*; *the rear gunner did not return fire & the machine carried on apparently under control.* I *broke off the attack & returned to base*". *Sgt Dennis Noble"*. Dennis took charge of Hurricane **N7366** for this epic flight an 'X plot' timed at 12.45hrs. After a rather bumpy landing due to the craters, B flight were refuelled & rearmed, & sent straight back into the air at 13.30hrs. B flights mechanics were now obtaining a turn around time of ten minutes.

17th August 1940, a fine sunny day, surprising enough one would have thought the Luftwaffe would have made excruciating attacks but nothing materialised. Giving ground staff time valuable time to patch up damage from the previous days bombing. "However there was one incident that took place proving the strength & durability of the Hurricane frame beyond its relative design limits". **Sgt Hallowes** had been on patrol with blue flight at 30.000 ft when he spotted below at around 12.000 ft what appeared to be an enemy plane, pushing the control column forward he dived towards the unsuspecting Dornier 17 pencil bomber, firing his guns he soon silenced the gunners & saw pieces of the fuselage falling away. In all the excitement he had forgotten that his engine was at full throttle & the Hurricanes wings were bending under the stress, fabric was being torn from away from the ailrons causing the aircraft to respond abnormally. He tried to pull out of the dive but the controls were under so much pressure from the speed being achieved so promptly he decided to use the trimming wheel, this had the effect of pushing the tail down therefore giving the aircraft a slow but decisive rising attitude. After gaining control he set course for home. His Hurricane bore all the marks of being over stressed with a distinctive bend in the wings, later Hawker technicians were sent to view the structure & decided that to have caused so much distortion the Hurricane must have exceeded 620 mph, far exceeding its limits. Sunday 18th August attacks were made on Ford, Gosport & Thorney Island airfields also the transmitter mast of the Chain Home (CH) station at Poling Sussex. Dennis was soon scrambled at 09.30hrs again at 12.55hrs & 14.10 this time flying **P3179**. After only 20 minutes into his first flight he was forced to return to base with his guns inoperative. Meanwhile as the mechanics repaired the problem he was ordered back up into the air in Hurricane **P3903**. As soon as the guns had been repaired on P3179 Dennis's trusty steed was placed into the capable hands of **Squadron leader J.V.C (tubby) Badger,** to continue the afternoon's activities. Finally, at the end of the day his logbook read, "Attacked formation of Ju 87s after first burst

The guns stopped, received bullet hole in each wing".
Monday 19th August a day consisting of only one flight at 15.30-15.40. Also a day of just sitting about waiting for the telephone to ring with orders to scramble.
Dennis took this opportunity to write to his sister Phylis; in his letter he describes his animosity towards the increasing air battles, & continues to explain his activities over the past few weeks in a very personal manner to his family, including his personal feelings.
Dennis's letter to Phylis indicates the tiredness felt by himself & the ground crews within the squadron, maybe the incident when his guns jammed on18th August, the responsible, rigger thought he had checked every thing but due to tiredness miscalculated his judgements.

Increasing amounts of completed combat reports, kept Intelligence Officers busy, all the facts & correctness of pilots claims for enemy aircraft destroyed had to be verified.
Two pilots claiming for the same aircraft destroyed, brings confusion to accurate detail reporting, a true picture of enemy loses had to be prepared to ascertain, perhaps with some guess work involved the German bomber & fighter strength that could be sent over the channel the next day.
Meanwhile, although Dennis had a quiet day, German intruders showed no signs of relaxing their attacks, as **Frank Carey** was about to find out, when he found himself in the thick of the fighting. He fired at a Junkers Ju 87 Stuka dive-bomber ahead of him, it immediately dived with flames pouring from the engine, the thick grey smoke loomed towards him as he headed towards the thick plume of smoke. He recalls being hit in the right knee, possibly from a stray round from another Hurricane attacking its prey a hazard during combat. Frank Carey unable to control his aeroplane, owing to his wound & damage sustained crashed at Pulbourgh Sussex.

Sgts Mess,
RAF STATION
TANGMERE
Sussex.
19-8-40
Dear Phyl,

Sorry that I have not written before, but I have had so little spare time during the past few weeks, and I always feel so dead tired when I am off duty.

I expect that Ma has already told you that I am with a fighter squadron on the South coast and what a hot spot it is too. We are the busiest sector in the group at the moment. For five days, a week we have to stay on the camp all day, and the sixth is free for us to go out where we please. Even so we never get away on time the Hun has a bad habit of having raids about a quarter to one, which means that a couple of hours hard work and a late dinner. Our day is from one o'clock to one o' clock, and so I am able to get to London and spend the evening with Marie, it makes a very pleasant and welcome break

We work more or less 24 hours a day and it is tiring, when we are not intercepting raids, we are patrolling convoys and believe me it is pretty hard going. Anyway I like it all the same plenty of larking about which suits me to the ground. I still fly Hurricanes and would not change for anything; I think that they are marvellous machines and would do anything in one. The first day I went into battle I was shot down, I had seven holes in the machine but I was Ok, One bullet went into the radiator which caused the coolant to leak and I came down with streams of white smoke from the engine. I was covered in the stuff, anyway I learned more in those few minutes than ever before, it was a fine experience. I shot down my first machine last Friday, a dive-bomber. The day before seven of us shot down a lone bomber, as there were seven of us no 0ne could hardly claim it. Yesterday I attacked another dive-bomber and as I was about to shoot the decisive blow my guns failed to work. Fortunately, I was able to dive away before I was caught napping, but I got a bullet in the wing. All that was due to the carelessness of a rigger who had failed to check the air system. I played hell when I came down. When I went up again they had gone. I know that Lionel has been on leave; I expect he was ready for it too. I hope that you both had a nice time.

I must close now Phyl so cheers and all the best.

Your loving brother DENNIS

OPERATIONS RECORD BOOK

From 1830 hrs 29/8/40 To 31/8/40 By B Flight 43 Squadron No of pages used for day

Aircraft type	Crew	Duty	Time up	Time down	Remarks
Hurricane					
V7366	PO Gorrie		1830	1900	RT Test
P3466	Sgt Hurry		1945	2000	RT Test
30. 8 40					
V6548	S/Ldr Badger		1125	1210	}
V7366	PO Gorrie		1125	1210	}
P3179	**Sgt Noble**		1125	1210	}
N7206	PO Upton		1125	1210	}
P3903	PO Du Vivier		1125	1210	}
P3466	Sgt Hurry		1125	1210	}
V6549	S/Ldr Bader		1655	1735	
V7366	PO Gorrie		1655	1735	X/ PLOT
P3466	Sgt Hurry		1655	1800	
V7206	PO Upton		1655	1800	}
P3905	PO Du Vivier		1655	1755	}
R5188	Sgt Barrow		1655	1755	}
P3386	Sgt Alying		2320	2359	Night Operation Patrol

Sgt Hallowes made an incredible contribution to the war effort on the 18th august 1940 with a remarkable achievement that perhaps could be considered impossible.

In his words "I caught up with a formation of Ju 87s line astern I opened fire at 300 yards two baled out of number five aircraft & a further two from the number four machine both aircraft fell into a steep dive & finally crashed four miles off Thorney Island".

Sgt Hallowes had done the impossible he had shot down both aircraft with one burst from his guns, an accomplishment that did not occur very often. However he had not finished yet, finding another enemy machine to attack, he fired another short burst this time cutting his selected German machine in half, braking its back just forward of the tail, it finally crashed in the Solent.

On his return to base Hallowes spotted a lone Hurricane closing in on a Stuka dive bomber, but unknown to its pilot a Messerschmitt Bf 109 was on its tail, promptly he lined himself up for a beam attack on the Me 109, firing his guns he could see the bullets raking the machine from nose to tail as it sped south 100yards in front, on his return he claimed the Me 109 as damaged in his report. It was much later in the day when reports started coming through that a Me 109 had crashed landed, on the Isle of Wight & with bullet holes from nose to tail, Sgt Hallowes had forced **Oberst Julius Newmann** to crash land & become a POW & after the war the two became friends. Jim Hallowes died 20th October 1987 & is buried in St Andrews churchyard Tangmere.

For the next three days 20th-23rd August 1940 the weather deteriorated, Rain & low cloud being the problem but with a few bright spells to the East. This gap in the weather gave the Germans a chance to send small forces to bomb West Malling, Manston, & Eastchurch airfields in Kent. 43 squadron were mostly grounded but did manage to investigate oncoming raiders at 14.40-15.35 hrs.

Saturday 24th August bright sunshine was the order of the day. Forty-threes pilots were up & about early waiting at dispersal areas. Perhaps reading a letter from home or just enjoying the morning sun, before the inevitable rush.

B Flight were ordered airborne twice throughout the day with no enemy contact materializing, could this have been due to the fact that Ventnor Radar station was temporally out of action following yesterdays raids. At 21.15hrs Dennis was ordered to practice night flying, Where he would have observed raging fires in Portsmouth docks. As dusk fell blue flames flowed majestically past the cockpit from the exhaust, he was obliged to locate his where-a-bouts in twilight without ground lights to assist due to the blackout, It would have made Navigating in the dark tricky, generating a completely different approach to flying; He landed back at Tangmere at 23.00hrs & he was I would imagine completely exhausted. Sunday 25th August & during the weekend 43 Squadron flew 67 combat hours, 11 of those at night, something of an achievement as they were almost on constant readiness or airborne patrolling the coast. Before the Germans could land troops onto the beaches they needed full air superiority, so bombardment of RAF airfields in the hope of demoralizing pilots & supporting crews continued. One of the most important factors that the Germans overlooked was the sheer determination of the Few, defending the coast was the uppermost objective. This was Britain's final defence position & must be held at all cost, not since the battle of Hastings in 1066 had England come so close to being invaded. The Battle of Britain was the most decisive conflict British people have had to face. Luftwaffe fighters could only give escort to bombers for 20 minutes over England, before returning to their bases in Normandy 350 miles away & with only a range of 400 miles the Germans needed to move their bases closer. Soon Me 110s from JG-2 based at Amiens & Me 109s from Le-Harve provided full cover to the bombers so they could reach further inland than ever before. Dennis was scrambled twice throughout the day but he recorded no combat activity, most likely, the raiders were using hit & run tactics. One reason was to draw up RAF fighters so that Me109s flying higher could pounce onto the unsuspecting Spitfires & Hurricanes as they made altitude. 'Britain could ill afford the losses as they were out numbered three to one'.

As aircraft production was slow, Fighter Command decided it would be more effective to hold back the Hurricanes in reserve to destroy the enemy bombers, rather than attack German fighters. One reason for this decision was that the Spitfire's eight Browning machine guns were directed to fire towards a central point causing almost definite destruction when hit, where as the Hurricanes eight Browning machine guns, were each directed to fire in a straight line producing a much wider spread across the surface area of the target, the aim was to inflict as much damage to the target as possible rather than achieve all out destruction. Obversely better if a target was destroyed but given the amount of damage a two second burst could achieve, perhaps to an engine or another part of the airframe, it could ground a bomber for a few day's. Strategically it would mean fewer bombs reaching their targets.

Monday 26th August was a cloudy day with most of the activity confined to Kent, attacks on Biggin Hill & Kenley & later during the afternoon raiders bombed Portsmouth Docks & Warmwell airfield in Dorset.

Wednesday 28th August, a day of comparatively little action in the South. **Squadron leader Badger** was asked to supply a pilot to ferry Hurricane **V7321** to Hatfield, he decided to send Dennis on this short pleasure flight, nevertheless one that could be dangerous, as he would have to pass over anti aircraft guns along the way hoping no-one got trigger-happy. It was possible to make a flight-plan avoiding the guns as much as possible, by planning a route via Fairoaks then on to Northholt to Hatfield still possible for the15 minute flight logged. He could for once take this as a sort of pleasure flight enjoying the countryside with patchwork fields below. His logbook recalls the flight in **P3179** but pencilled in over the top is **V7321** a mistake made as he had been flying constantly in P3179. Hatfield was the base for De Havilland & could have suggested a propeller change to the new Constant speed type, improving the Rolls-Royce Merlin output.

On Thursday 29th August 1940, a reasonably fine day was forecast, & the fine weather kept 43 squadron active all day.

No action was reported even though the squadron had flown 13 sorties throughout the day. Dennis once again flew his trusty steed **P3179;** unbeknown to him the following day was to be his last. **Friday 30th August 1940** was a wonderful sunny day with a few Cumulus clouds around at 5000-8000 ft. a day when the Luftwaffe geared up for a maximum effort flying 1345 sorties. No entry was made in Dennis's logbook except that of another hand reading "Killed in Action" possibly the C/O, one more question that is worthy of note is that in the Operations record book for 43 squadron it clearly states, Sgt Noble Killed (Involved in Battle Accident at Hove)

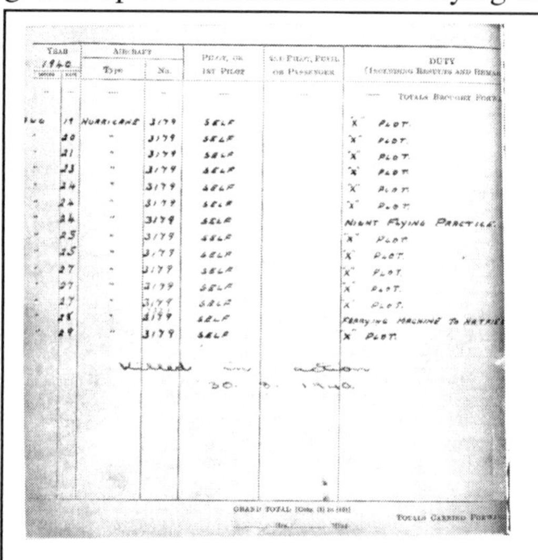

Year 1940		Aircraft Type	No.	Pilot, or 1st Pilot	2nd Pilot, Pupil or Passenger	Duty (Including Results and Remarks)
						Totals Brought Forward
Aug	19	Hurricane	3179	Self		"X" Plot.
"	20	"	3179	Self		"X" Plot.
"	21	"	3179	Self		"X" Plot.
"	23	"	3179	Self		"X" Plot.
"	24	"	3179	Self		"X" Plot.
"	24	"	3179	Self		"X" Plot.
"	24	"	3179	Self		Night Flying Practice.
"	25	"	3179	Self		"X" Plot.
"	25	"	3179	Self		"X" Plot.
"	27	"	3179	Self		"X" Plot.
"	27	"	3179	Self		"X" Plot.
"	27	"	3179	Self		"X" Plot.
"	28	"	3179	Self		Ferrying machine to [illegible]
"	29	"	3179	Self		"X" Plot.

Killed in Action
30. 8. 1940.

Grand Total

Last entry in Sgt Nobles Logbook & Operations Record 43 Sqdn

R.A.F. Form 540. OPERATIONS RECORD BOOK Page No Five
Of unit or Formation 43 squadron No of Pages for day ....

PLACE	DATE	Summery of Events	References to Appendices
Tangmere	30-8-40	F/O Marshall posted to 43 squadron from RAF Tangmere for Intelligence Duties, P/O CRIDLAN Posted to HQ 12 Group for Intelligence Duties Flt MORGAN Discharged station sick quarters TANGMERE S/LDR BADGER Involved in F.B. at Birdham admitted to Ashford Hospital Posted N/E Tangmere. Sgt NOBLE Involved in Battle Accident at Hove (Killed).	

....

Sqdn Ldr G Lott Awarded the DSO. Sqdn Ldr Badger Awarded the DFC.
Flt Dalton Morgan awarded the DFC. P/O CA Woods-Scrawen Awarded DFC.
Sgt H.J.L. Hallowes Awarded the DFC and Bar.

COMRADES IN ARMS.

'For three weeks Sgt Dennis Noble became a Comrade in Arms' & to explain the gallantry produced by RAF crews during the Battle of Britain we should start with the ground crews, who bravely worked under immense pressure throughout air raids with long hours every day keeping the squadrons aircraft serviceable. In an interview with the Author **Bill Littlemore** recalls,

My memories of that period in August 1940 with 43 squadron as one of 'B' flights mechanics remain clear today even after all these years have passed. Up early in the morning & into ablutions then onto breakfast in the cookhouse followed by the walk to flight dispersal where ones Hurricane waited. Engine covers were removed mechanics; riggers & armourers were soon busy with their daily inspections, once the aircraft had been certified as airworthy Chiefy was informed & the Engineering Officer in turn. Then the squadrons status was reported to Number 11 group who would then bring us to standby for 30 minutes, from that we passed to readiness where from that point on we would wait for the panic bell, with the shout" start engines" the pilots hastily ran towards their machines, we would help them on with their parachutes & fasten the seat harness. Within seconds, the aerodrome would echo to the roar of Merlins as they thundered across the grass taking up formation positions, as they got airborne. For us on the ground the period of waiting began, all to often some of the Hurricanes did not return this bought anxious & seemingly interminable periods of waiting with fading hope, there were possibility's that a crew's pilot had landed away at another aerodrome to refuel.

'It is fallacy that grown men do not weep as many a tear was shed as one's pilot & aircraft failed to return, perhaps only minutes after checking & strapping in the pilot. Maybe he was a well known face around the airfield workshops, but a new pilot & Hurricane would soon take the place of the fallen & the rotation would start all over again"

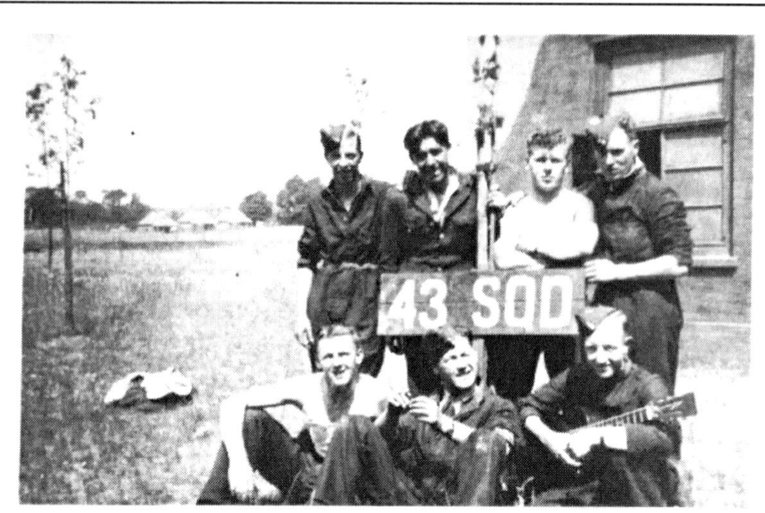

Ground Crew 'B' Flight 43 Squadron summer 1940,
Back Row, Pete Walters, Danny Wallace, Bill McKinlay, Ginger Wayne,
Front Row, Bill Stanger, Fred Dummer, Ernie Gatwick.

60 Year's on June 2000
Left to Right, Bill Littlemore, Dick Brown, & Bill McKinlay.

George Roberts. F/Mech.43 squadron Tangmere Known as Jack in the Squadron & Flt Mechanic to Squadron Leader Caesar HULL in fact the last person to strap Caesar Hull into his hurricane V6641 before he was killed on the 7th September 1940, along with his good friend Flt Dickie Reynell also shot down in the same action he fell dead in his parachute at Crown point Blackheath.

43 Squadron was formed at Stirling, Scotland in1916 & still operational today at St Leuchars flying GR3 Tornadoes & perhaps soon the Euro Fighter. 43 Squadron secured a history of Valour in the Field of Battle throughout two World Wars & were aptly branded the 'Fighting Cocks' some of these valiant airmen formed part of the squadron during the 1930s demonstrating their flying ability at the Hendon Air Pageants, a display of perfection unequalled by the average pilot. One such pilot was **P/O Caesar Hull** an experienced airman with a very flamboyant attitude to life, making people laugh with his jovial antics. He assumed command of the squadron at Tangmere on 31st August 1940, lasting only seven days as he was killed on 7th September 1940. On 3rd September 1939 **F/O J.I Kilmartin** became the squadrons first pilot to fire his guns air to air, he had been ordered to shoot down a barrage balloon that had escaped its moorings & was drifting from Portsmouth into the direction of Farnbourgh in fact three other pilots had similar experiences including Caesar Hull. Meanwhile **Squadron leader R.E Bain** was relinquishing command to **Squadron Leader George Lott,** before transferring 43 to Acklington Newcastle-upon-Tyne in January 1940. On one occasion Caesar Hull while on patrol with a flight spotted a lone German Heinkel 111 escaping into cloud & exchanged fire. On his return Caesars Hurricane was found to have received a bullet hole in the rear fuselage. Unexpectedly the same Heinkel was on reconnaissance patrol the next day, only to meet Caesar Hull again, this time he did not miss sending the Heinkel crashing into the sea, it's crew not even realising the Hurricane was the same fighter they had fired at the previous day. May 1940 arrived & 43 were ordered south once again to Tangmere, in the physically powerful leadership of Sqdn Ldr George Lott, pilots respected him for both his leadership & his sound advice. 'Right from Dennis's first days with the squadron he was given guidance from this fatherly figure who wore a patch over one eye' after an injury received on the 4th July 1940 when a cannon shell exploded against the screen of his Hurricane P3464 costing him the loss of one eye in action off

Littlehampton in Sussex. 'Despite excruciating pain & with his aircraft on fire he tried desperately to land back at Tangmere' but three miles from base the flames reached a critical stage & he abandoned the Hurricane at a dangerously low altitude of 700 feet. His machine crashed onto Fontwell Racecourse & burnt so fiercely that hardly anything was salvageable only the tail wheel survived intact this was given to one of the local people for his wheelbarrow.
George Lott relinquished his command of 43 Squadron to Squadron **Leader J.V.C (Tubby) Badger DFC**. The citation perhaps sums up the quality of this new leader.

"This Officer assumed command of a squadron in July 1940 & it is through his personal leadership that the squadron has achieved so many successes since the intensive air operations began. He has been instrumental in destroying six enemy aircraft in spite of the fact that on three separate occasions he has returned with his aircraft very badly damaged through enemy cannon fire. He has immediately taken off in another aircraft to lead his squadron on patrol. Squadron Leader Badger has displayed great courage & resolution".
Born in Lambeth 1911 after his mother had temporarily moved from Ireland. Attending Fountain Ville Primary School Belfast & the Royal Belfast Academical Institute, he graduated from Matriculated at Queens University Belfast. Then during 1928 he was accepted into the RAF at Halton as an Aero Engine Fitter, where he passed out as their top apprentice & was rewarded with a Cadetship at the Royal Airforce College Cranwell in1931. He graduated as their best all round Flight Cadet & was awarded the **Sword of Honour** by Air Vice Marshal Sir Robert Popham in July 1933.After a career incorporating time spent on HMS Courageous as a test pilot, earning him the Rank of Flight Lieutenant & with a total of 1373 flying hours, Badger was shot down 30th August 1940 only a few hours after Sgt Noble had been flying as his wingman **Green Two**.

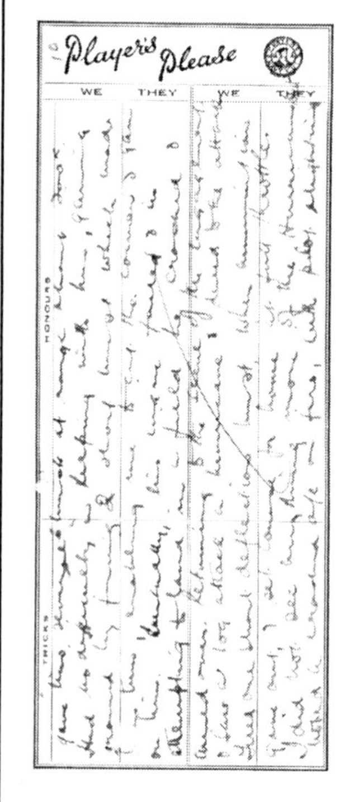

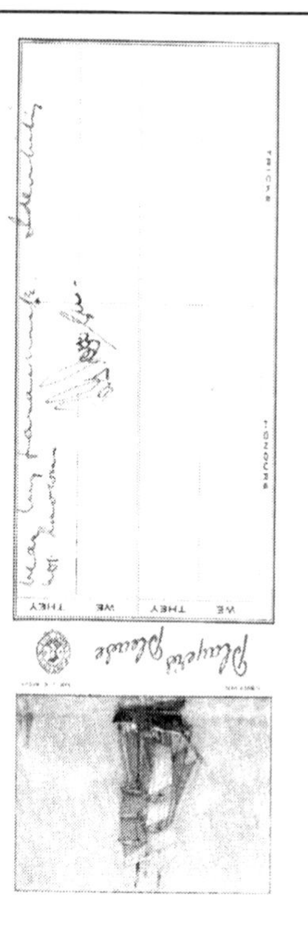

Written many years ago by Squadron leader George Lott describing an attack in 1940.

Gave him severe burst at range about 200ft had no difficulty keeping with him, gaining ground by firing short burst which made him turn enabling me to cut the corner & Gain on him eventually his engine failed& no attempt to land in a field he crashed & turned over. Returning to the scene of the engagement I saw a 109 attack a hurricane I dived to attack fired one short deflection burst when ammunition ran out. Set coarse for home at full throttle did not see anything more of the hurricane watched a crashed A/C on fire with pilot alighting by parachute Id not known.

Page from Squadron Ldr Badgers Log Book August 1940

YEAR 1940 DATE	AIRCRAFT Type	AIRCRAFT No.	PILOT, OR 1ST PILOT	2ND PILOT, PUPIL OR PASSENGER	(INCLUDING
8	HURRICANE	3971	SELF	-	35 "X" RAID BF…
8	—"—	3971	SELF	-	36 "X" RAID
8	—"—	3971	—"—	-	37 "X" RAID
9	—"—	3971	—"—	-	38 "X" RAID
10	—"—	3971	—"—	-	39 "X" RAID
11	—"—	3971	—"—	-	40 "X" RAID
11	—"—	3971	—"—	-	41 "X" RAID
11	—"—	3971	—"—	-	42 "X" RAID
11	—"—	3971	—"—	-	43 "X" RAID
12	—"—	3971	—"—	-	44 "X" RAID
12	—"—	3971	—"—	-	45 "X" RAID
13	—"—	3971	—"—	-	46 "X" RAID (2
13	—"—	3971	—"—	-	47 "X" RAID
14	—"—	3971	—"—	-	48 "X" RAID
14	—"—	3971	—"—	-	49 "X" RAID
14	—"—	3971	—"—	-	50 "X" RAID
15	—"—	3971	—"—	-	51 CONVOY PATR…
15	—"—	3971	—"—	-	52 "X" RAID
15	—"—	3971	—"— Sgt … listed in records	-	53 "X" RAID
16	—"—	(3424 3971	—"—	-	54 "X" RAID 3
16	—"—	3971)	—"—	-	55 "X" RAID
17	—"—	3903	—"—	-	56 "X" RAID
17	—"—	3903	—"—	-	57 "X" RAID

GRAND TOTAL [Cols. (1) to (10)]

Shortly after 17.30 hrs Squadron Leader Badger flying Hurricane **V6548** in action over Woodchurch Kent & his aircraft was crippled by enemy fire over an area known as Cole's Wood. He had no alternative but to abandon the stricken machine promptly he jumped taking to his parachute, an eyewitness testifies, "I saw the Hurricane coming down like a comet". Crashing into pastureland at Cuckoo's Corner Woodchurch, luckily no one was injured. Roy Blundell saw Badger floating helplessly earthwards when suddenly a Messerschmitt Bf 109 headed towards him selecting his machine guns the pilot fired a short burst towards the helpless figure falling slowly towards a group of trees. A murderous attack on a defenceless man, or was it a justifiable act of war? Opinions differ somewhat one RAF pilot who witnessed such an attack was so incensed that he chased the German responsible right over the channel shooting him down into the sea, and then circling to make sure that the German did not survive. Fighter Commands Sir Hugh Dowding commanded Number 16 Squadron RFC, in France during 1915 & was a fighter pilot himself. He took a pragmatic view that an enemy pilot parachuting onto British soil was in his opinion, certain to be captured & was in effect already a prisoner of war. However a pilot parachuting down into his own territory not only could, but would also most certainly rejoin his unit, which meant he would still be a combatant & could legitimately be shot & killed. As ever Dowding was a realist, none of which was of much comfort to tubby Badger now wounded & with much worse to come. Drifting towards Townland farm house, about a mile to the northeast of the village he noticed that he was in danger of landing on the roof, he struggled to steer the chute by pulling on the ropes, but unfortunately he landed in a row of Ash trees 10feet from the house coming to rest astride a forked branch smashing his pelvis in the process. The owner's wife **Mrs Mary Munton** heard the sound of splitting braches & dashed outside to investigate. Finding the trees damaged by this unconventional trespasser seated in them, she did not stop to think instead she gave Badger a tongue

Lashing before realising that he was hurt. Badger was then carefully retrieved & given a glass of whisky & a local lady **Nurse Jordan** gave emergency first aid. On his arrival at Ashford Hospital, he insisted on sending a telegram to the squadron giving details of the engagements he had participated in during the day, including the action in which Dennis Noble was killed. It is distasteful to record that at the height of the Battle of Britain a wounded hero could be robbed. However it happened, in this instance Squadron Leader Badger had been given a gold watch for his 21st birthday & was believed to be wearing it when he landed. It was missing by the time he arrived at the hospital along with his boots, Local legend has it that one of the villagers who rescued Badger from the trees was a fanatical watch collector & repairer, whether or not temptation had proved too great, or perhaps the watch was simply torn off during the hectic commotion, alas this incident was not forgotten in the village for many years & doubts were cast which can sometimes be a very cruel judgment. **P/O George Wellard** of 607 Squadron was witness to Badgers courage he recalled " After being shot down I was in Ashford hospital another inmate was Squadron Leader Badger DFC of 43 Squadron He had split his pelvis after baling out & there was nothing that could be done. During the whole time until he died he laughed & joked with all the nurses & visitors as though he would live forever". Even the great spirit of this brave gentleman could not triumph over his internal injuries. Ten agonising months after his combat he finally surrendered to his wounds, he died on 30th June 1941. 'Almost as a last act as commanding officer of 43 squadron he found time to file his reports for the 30th August 1940 & send a telegram to the parents of Sgt Noble. " A devoted & true leader", a man of great character & a pilot of exceptional ability would be needed to succeed him. Such a man would be **Squadron leader Caesar Hull,** as we have seen earlier in this chapter he was a very capable aviator & leader, but he too met a fate that many of his friends previously had given their lives for 'Freedom'.

Commanding 43 for only one week as on the 7th September 1940, the squadron scrambled with Caesar leading a formation of nine Hurricanes. According to reports he was still standing in the cockpit as he raced across the grass preparing for take off giving substance to the amount of haste needed. They were vectored onto a force of Dornier 17s crossing the channel at 18000ft with Messerschmitt 110s, 500ft above them & Me 109s at 25000ft, mere silver dots in the sunshine. Caesar Hull kept his flight above the bombers at 1500ft to reach an advantage point. Bombers were reaching the outskirts of London by the time Caesar arrived shouting over the radio 'Tally Ho' as contact was made. Over the radio he told **Flt Lt Kilmartin** to keep his section trailing behind & to watch out for Enemy fighters. Caesar Hulls wingman **Sgt C.A.L Hurry** reported saying that Caesar had dived astern a Dornier 17 & then pulled out to make a synchronised beam attack he was reported to say "I raked the bomber from one end to the other & broke away underneath when I turned to come in again their was no sign of anyone else". There are many ways of dying. Some men like Dennis Noble pass on silently, 'some die with a curse on their lips' & 'some die singing but Caesars last words over the radio were "Sail in & Smash them. Accompanied by his characteristically deep throaty chuckle. He was discovered unrecognisable in the Cockpit of his Hurricane **V6641** that had burnt out in the playing field of Purley Grammar School where today stands the buildings of Coulsdon College. Only the serial Numbers of his 303 Browning Machine Guns identified the aeroplane. Yet, a fence at the bottom of the gardens still bears scars of the impact fire. Also in this engagement was his life long friend Australian Hawker test pilot **Flt Lt Richard Carew Reynell,** "Dickie" as he was known throughout the squadron had been one of the display pilots demonstrating the Hawker Fury, his skills especially on the Hurricane led to him becoming a Hawker Test pilot. 'Pilots in the squadron were diminishing rapidly & it was necessary to redeploy pilots such as 'Dickie Reynell', transferred from non-operational duties. Was it a twist of fate that

The farmer took this photograph of Squadron Ldr Tubby Badger descending in his parachute minutes before he landed in Ash trees just feet away from the farmhouse

TOP, Ash trees in which Squadron Leader Badger landed after baling out of his stricken aircraft 30th August 1940, BELOW crash site at Cuckoos Corner Woodchurch of V6548.

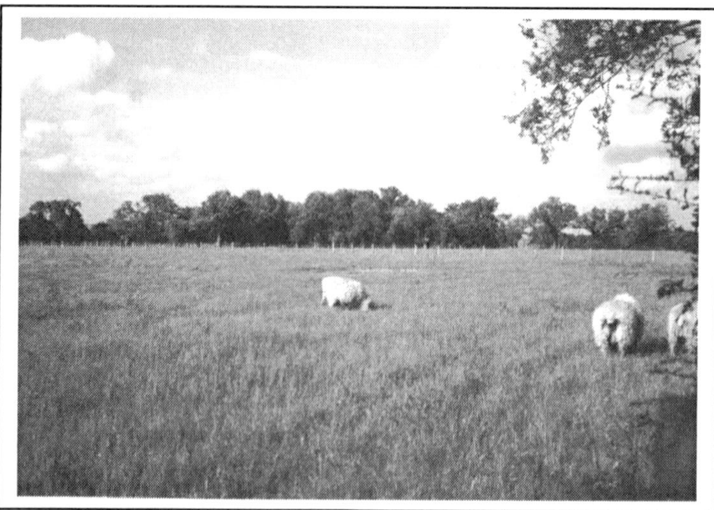

TOWNLAND FARM.
1941

Dear MR Badger.

I must write you a line to tell you how dreadfully grieved I am to see the death of your son in todays Times. You will not know who I am but it was in my garden that your son landed when his machine was hit and he had to take to his parachute. He was so badly wounded that their was little we could do for him.
His courage was apsolutly amazing and I shall never forget it. I saw him a few times when he was in Ashford hostpitial and though he was ill he was always brave and smiling.
Please do not bother to reply to this but I did want to send you my sympathy.

Yours sincerely
Mary F Munton

This letter was sent to the father of Squadron leader J.V.C *Badger by the farmers wife of Townland farm, Ashford Kent*

This picture was taken Midday on 7th September 1940 outside the Officers Mess RAF Tangmere. Caesar Hull & Dickie Reynell were both killed two hours later.
L to R F/O Derrick Upton. F/O Marshall Intelligence Officer. Sqdn Ldr Caesar Hull. C/O Sqdn Ldr George Lott. P/O Frank Carey. Flt Dickie Reynell. F/O Gorrie. Station Commander RAF Tangmere W/CDR Jack Boret. F/O Kilmartin last an unknown Army Officer.

That on the 7th September 1940 both Dickie Reynell & Caesar Hull were killed within two hours of sharing a well earned 'refreshing beer' together as a part of a leisurely group of friends enjoying a moment of tranquillity absorbing in the Sussex Sunshine. Just before his death, Dickie Reynell was heard on his radio, asking for the position of his squadron. The next news that reached communications was that he had fallen to earth at Grey Ladies Blackheath, after his parachute had malfunctioned. By grim Co-incidence his was the third death in the squadron that month, & only 'one week' into September, some were attributable to parachute accidents. The first being the death of **F/O P.P Woods-Scawen 85** Squadron. One of two brothers serving in fighter command. He was killed 1st September 1940 due to parachute failure, after baling out of Hurricane P3150 at Kenley. 2nd September 1940, 43 squadron were scrambled at 12.45 hrs to intercept enemy formations gathering over the North Kent Coast, in this action P/O **Tony Woods-Scawen,** in Hurricane **V7420** had been damaged by enemy fire & set alight, he attempted to make a forced landing but the flames became so intense, he decided to bale out. It was the same parachute he had cautiously carried out of France after baling out there on 10th June 1940.This time though it failed to deploy fully & he was killed instantly after plummeting to earth at Ivychurch Kent, not knowing that his brother had been killed hours before. One man who had served through 'peace & war' was **F/O Frank Carey,** this resolute young man of 43 squadron originally joined in 1927, the year in which '43' became the first peace time residents of Tangmere, flying Gloster Gamecock biplanes two years before they were re-equipped with the first all metal aircraft to enter service with the RAF, these were Armstrong Whitworth Siskin. During 1937 he flew with the squadron team at Hendon Air pageant where he retained the best overall distance in the landing competition flying a Hawker Hart. The competition requires the machine to be flown over a fixed wire & landing in a prescribed distance.

Frank Carey did not get the official accolade for his performance, because a protest was lodged, but 43squadron always believed that their man had won fair & square. In a personal interview with Keith Arnold (Author) during 1997, Frank Carey expressed his interpretation towards night flying in the Hawker Fury. 'Pilots were expected to be both diurnal & nocturnal however none of the Fury's carried anything that even vaguely resembled night flying fitments, designed as daytime interceptors & this probably led to the RAF expression 'Birds & Bloody fools fly – Bats & Bloody fools fly by night' Frank recalled that in the night role we were rather badly placed, "For instance the Fury did not have landing lights vital at that time as one could not communicate & request landing permission. There was also no cockpit illumination, but someone did come up with an ingenious idea that if we tied torches to the Port longhorn it would be a step towards a problem solved. Another major inconvenience was when throttling back we were immediately blinded by the flames from the Rolls-Royce Kestrel engines short exhaust stubs, when landing the ground looms up at an alarming rate making it quite dramatic especially just before the wheels touch down". Frank Carey luckily did not have to fly the Fury in anger because when war was declared 3 September 1939. 43 squadron were equipped with Hurricanes with a full range of instrumentation built in as standard. 43 squadron aircraft now all brandished the new squadron codes F.T. instead of N.Q. that previously identified them. They found themselves in solitude at Tangmere' as No 1 squadron had been ordered to France. Soon afterwards 43 squadron prepared for a move to Accrington on the 16th November 1939. Twenty miles from Newcastle –upon-Tyne, from one end of the country to the other & what a difference in climate with cold winds coming in from Siberia made the airfield a cold bleak location. Frank Carey flew his first operational sortie from this snow-covered airfield 29th January 1940. He & **P/O North** flew beside Caesar Hull in the unsuccessful interception of a Heinkel 111, which ended in the German crew claiming to have shot down Hull's Aircraft.

Therefore, it was appropriate that Frank Carey flew as Caesar's wingman the following day giving substance to the claim of a Heinkel destroyed at Phyllis Wood, Treyford, the same one that had reported Hulls Hurricane destroyed. This time however there were two reports of the combat, with Frank Carey sharing the Heinkel with Caesar Hull. Three weeks later, he was awarded the DFM. Frank was commissioned In March leaving the squadron to join No 3 at Kenley Surrey. 'In May 1940 Frank Carey accompanied No 3 squadron to Melville France to fend off German bombers devastating the French & British Armies. During this ill fated operation he destroyed a Heinkel 111 which went into a dive vertically & plunged into the ground killing it's crew, but not before a gunner with a Mg 15 had fired a few rounds into Careys Hurricane. German gunners were brave men who seldom retreated from the possible chance of retaliating, Frank Carey was not the only pilot to suffer from return fire it seems that Dennis Noble was also a victim. By the end of March Frank Carey had a Tally of 11 confirmed victories & several probables. With resistance in France coming to an end & German troops entering Paris 14th June 1940. No 3 squadron were ordered to return to England two days later. After a short rest Frank was sent back to rejoin 43 squadron & on the squadrons return from Wick Scotland, Frank soon made up for lost time when on 9th July he destroyed a Me110 followed by a Me 109 ten day's later. Then on the 8th August he was slightly wounded, but managed to get even four days later, once again destroying two Junker 87s on the 16 &18th August whilst leading A Flight into action over Selsey Bill, Sussex. He reported "I fired at one ahead of me when it stood up on it's nose with flames coming out of it, then all of a sudden I was hit in the knee by cross fire or a stray bullet from another Hurricane, I eventually crash landed at Pulborough". Frank required a short stay in hospital in a ward that became known as Forty Threes because of the increasing amount of injured pilots residing there. For his experience & courage during the Battle of Britain he was awarded the DFC & Bar, when his wounds had healed he was transferred to the Far East where he continued to give the enemy hell. In a personal letter to Keith Arnold (Author) early in 1998, Frank Carey remembers a few of the experiences he faced while serving in France. "I was shot down 14th May 1940 at Grey-Doiccon South East of Brussels, I immediately tried to make my way home by a mixture of walking & and had the experience of riding in a 1914 World War One Crossley Ambulance. We soon arrived at a succession of tents, near to a children's school close to Dieppe, which had been requisitioned as a hospital. From here I was evacuated further into France by hospital train & that was soon bombed with half its coaches damaged or on fire. Eventually we continued our journey towards the Atlantic Ocean, feeding off bread & wine that was put out on railway stations for the benefit of fugitives like ourselves fleeing from the Hun. We eventually reached La Baule near St Nazaire a fellow wounded pilot. I was soon discharged to a tented RAF depot near Nantes. There two RAF pilots both in similar condition joined us. Realising that if we wanted to return home we would have to save ourselves & overhearing a conversation of an abandoned Bristol Bombay high wing twin engine transport plane that was apparently doing nothing, we found it & cleaned it up, very roughly though & filled it with French airforce petrol. There seemed no reason why I could not fly, so on the 6th June 1940 we left France in this bright yellow 'Target' on a very sunny day we stood out for miles. Fortunately we met no resistance from the Luftwaffe, but we had cause for some concern when the RAF came to have a look at us. We eventually landed at Hendon after a 330-mile flight & a few days later I returned to 43 squadron at Tangmere, where I learned that I had been awarded the DFC & Bar. 'Although the citation quoted the name & number of the innocent pilot Officer who had been sitting quietly nr Bristol all the time & interfering with no body! When leaving France in rather a hurry I left behind my pilots logbook & all my personal kit, unfortunately this also happened later in the war while I was commanding an air fighting training unit in Calcutta". Frank Carey reached the rank of Group

Captain before retiring after a very distinguished career. He is known to have destroyed 28 Enemy planes with 12 probable, but on several occasions his personal effects went astray when Japanese overran RAF airfields. This brave & resourceful Officer who started his career on the lowest rung of the ladder soon reached higher grades than most of his contemporaries. Having to piece together his career from memory or from a few documents remaining, there is reason to believe that his total score was in the region of 33 destroyed. Increasing two more Bar's to his Distinguished Flying Cross this proves that he is indeed an Ace amongst Aces.

Another famous face with a name that continually comes to the forefront is that of **Sgt Herbert James Lampriere Hallowes** whose technique frequently went unobserved. A former RAF Apprentice who served with 43 squadron, from the first day of War & there after he always seemed to be where the action was. Dennis Noble flew along side him into battle on several occasions Hallowes was a pilot with the DFM proudly pinned on his tunic. By the time the Battle of Britain was over he had a tally of 19 victories with more success awaiting him during the winter months. By 31 January 1941, he was rated as third in the list of British Ace's with 21 Victories. Just ahead were two other famous names **P/O J.H Lacey, (Ginger)** with 23 destroyed & **P/O E.S Lock DSO, DFC & Bar** with at least 22, tragically he was killed in action in the spring of 1941. Trailing behind at this stage, were **"Sailor" Malan, & Robert Stanford Tuck** both with the DFC, DSO & Bar with 18 victories each. **Sgt Charles Albert Henry Ayling** joined 43 squadron in 1939 & was one of ten pilots who participated in a sortie over France on 7th June 1940 only to be shot down by the Luftwaffe, his Hurricane being so badly damaged that he crash landed at Rouen France, Resourcefully he managed to get away from Garney aerodrome in an abandoned Hurricane in which the port wing tank had been punctured, there after he served with 43 until posted to 66 squadron at Kenley, he was killed in his Spitfire at Newchurch 11th October 1940.

Group Captain Frank Carey 1997.

ONE OF THE FEW.

Sgt Alex Hurry 43 Sqdn, B Flight.

Sgt Hurry was in action with B flight when Sgt Noble was killed 30th August 1940.

The reverse of this picture it is inscribed

To Bill from your old comrade Alex Hurry

Dennis made only a few friends within the squadron, as it was almost impossible due to one's tiredness of constant readiness at dispersal. Two pilots who shared their time with him were **Flt Officer Van den Hove.** He flew one of 15 hurricanes that reached operational service with the Belgium airforce before the invasion of his Country. Then in May 1940 Van den hove, went into France only to be trapped once again, when the French surrendered to the Germans on 21st June 1940. He & another Belgium pilot made their bid for freedom to Port Vendes a small Mediterranean port. Eventually they were picked up by a British Destroyer & transferred to a Convoy heading to England. After a short rest he was posted to 43 Squadron, receiving a commission on the 5th August 1940. During an attack on Tangmere on the 16th August he destroyed a Ju 87 Stuka, with a further two victories one on 26th August when a Me Bf 109e fell to his guns, then a Me110 on 4th September, in this action his glycol tank suffered a hit causing a mid air fire forcing him to land at Ford aerodrome. He was posted to 501 Squadron Kenley on the 11th September but four days after joining he was killed when his Hurricane exploded over Ashford Kent, & ended up in the river Stour. This happened during an engagement with a Dornier 17, it was believed that escorting fighters had attacked him. His compatriot **P/O Albert le Roy Du-Vivier** was also an experienced pilot escaping from France with him, & enchantingly the French had posted him as a Deserter. With limited flying time he converted to Hurricanes as previously he had only flown Fait CR42s & Fairey Firefly's. Posted to 43 Squadron Tangmere from 5 O.T.U. on 4th August. He destroyed a Ju 87 on the 16th August, but after a fight with Me Bf109s on 2nd September he suffered leg wounds baling out from his Hurricane. On his return to the squadron in October he was promoted to Flight Commander & ironically after all the times that he faced death throughout the war, he finally fell victim to a road accident in America during the 1980s whilst riding a Motor Cycle. There were many brave acts of heroism performed during the summer of 1940 & this chapter has been a tribute to just several of the Few.

Out of the Strain of the Doing – Into the Peace of the Done.

August 30th 1940, the smell of damp grass is carried on the morning breeze, smoke from the chimney of the N.A.A.F.I canteen spirals into the sky gently giving way to the hustle & bustle of a front line aerodrome. Pilots make their way to allocated dispersal areas & as the sun rises slowly in the morning sky riggers & mechanics are still working on the 'lame ducks ' from earlier battles. Armourers hastily re-arm the Hurricanes & check the eight browning machine guns. Finally sticking cloth patches over the gun ports preventing dust or other objects entering the barrels causing malfunction. Several pilots gaze into the blue sky wondering if they would return to fight tomorrow, or would they join the increasing ranks of yesterday's fallen comrades. Thoughts of loved ones back home. "Did I finish writing my letter home last night or did I fall asleep," One such pilot was Dennis Noble soon to join the ranks of the fallen.
A fine day was forecast for the South of England therefore heavy attacks could be guaranteed. RAF aerodromes were placed on high readiness, Biggin Hill, Kenley, & Hawkinge were all suffering, but at 11.15 hrs it became Tangmeres turn to make contact with the enemy. The battle cry scramble 'B' flight echoed over the dispersal. Dennis made haste towards his Hurricane **P3179** putting on his parachute & being helped into the cockpit by his mechanic who was explaining any small defects or symptoms he would have to observe regarding the Hurricane's temperament.
As they took off 11.20 the operations room directed them to assist the already airborne 'A' flight, a large formation of bombers was heading for the coast at Brighton. 'B' flight consisted of **Squadron leader "Tubby" Badger, P/O Du Vivier, P/O Upton, P/O Gorrie & Sgt Hurry;** Dennis was to fly as 'Green two' Badger's wingman. Climbing to 10,000 feet they set course towards the enemy. 'Meanwhile residents of Hove were going about there normal every day activities, not taking very much notice of the air battle raging just off the coast. Just another Battle' something they

were about to endure was the proximity of the raging battle, & would soon be involved with reality of war on one's own door step. Midday approached with the sun for a moment hiding behind fluffy grey & white clouds, they could see the attacking planes & hear the rattle of their machine guns. Drawing nearer could be seen the bomber formations heading towards the coast, with some formations already heading inland. RAF Hurricanes were darting through the formations firing at selected targets; the loud wailing of a siren sounds its warning & town's folk race for the shelters. A number of people not heeding the warning would gaze skywards watching the dogfights. Dramatically at 11.58 hrs an aeroplane was seen to dive almost vertically & within seconds crashed with a thunderous explosion into the pavement of Woodhouse Road, Hove, on the junction of Portland Road. At this point it was clear that the stricken aircraft was a fighter but it was still unknown exactly what had happened. Let's take up the story from eye witness accounts where later we can dissect the facts using the knowledge of professional data, from information discovered during the recovery in 1996 from the aeroplane itself. The **Reverend John Watts** a schoolboy at the time. He recalls "*That morning I had gone along the seafront at Hove with my father, suddenly we noticed a group of bystanders looking upwards & out to sea, we naturally followed suit & saw a couple of Hurricanes climbing rapidly to intercept a group of Messerschmitts & flew into a cloud as if to chase them out. Meanwhile a second Hurricane sped around the cloud I suppose this manoeuvre could be to obtain a position to catch enemy aircraft coming out from the cloud. One behind the other in a steep dive we could hear the guns firing from the rear aircraft & everyone started cheering someone shouted hurrah you've got one; but suddenly as the plane dived earthwards we could see it was a Hurricane being machine gunned & we were all stunned to silence. It never pulled out of its dive but finally disappeared behind buildings. The Messerschmitt followed it to* *at a low altitude & with what seemed some difficulty pulled out of the dive & flew away"*

Another witness **Eric Masters** quoted in the Evening Argus news paper " *at the time he was shot down the sky was full of bombers approximately 200, although you could not see much as the sun was bright. Then a massive ball of flame & smoke it really shook me up I have never forgotten it".*

Tony Martlew a 12 year old boy standing on the Downs had a much wider view of the situation. *"I was at home as it was the school holiday's I heard a dog fight going on & I went into the garden to watch, there were many aircraft involved possibly more than a hundred the noise was tremendous with the sound of engines & gunfire. I saw one plane falling straight down to earth like an arrow".* From an vantage point at Slonk Hill **Chris Martin** reported, *"I was helping troops dig slit trenches when we all stopped the solders started cheering it was a hell of a battle I saw a plane diving at first I though it was a Messerschmitt as we all did but it was actually a Hurricane with the Messerschmitt chasing it there were almost vertical puffs of smoke were coming from it's guns, & the Hurricane continued straight down, The next thing was a plume of smoke I can picture it now, & hear the engine screaming, we were all very subdued as one of our pilots must have been killed".*

We must consider the relative position of Slonk Hill. It was three miles or more away from where the battle raged therefore aeroplanes over Hove would appear very small & it would be hard to identify one fighter from another, with many planes scurrying about all over the sky. Nevertheless one would have been able to see two planes diving & one crash into the town & make the likely assumption that the one trailing was a Messerschmitt .

Letters & Telephone calls from sources claiming to have seen the action over Hove started to get unsuitable in substance. It was now time to piece together those which were completely inaccurate & those with some form of likelihood. 'People believe what they see or hear' but after 56 years or more evidence can be confused as

The mind almost certainly plays tricks on a well-told family story sometimes leading to slight exaggeration, or perhaps distortion. Two more eyewitnesses reported seeing the pilot baling out to safety, another reported flames coming from the cockpit & thought that the pilot had baled out & went on to say that British pilots were circling the parachute to give added protection.

Leo Cruttenden then 11 years old remembers seeing the plane come down from his home in Dyke Road Brighton. " *My 'fathers' firm had a war office excavation contract & he had sent a team down to dig out the tail section, I seem to remember him saying that it was a Spitfire not a Hurricane".*

It would appear from these accounts that a picture of what actually happened is very hard to reveal. Some of the facts indicate that the weather was bright with clouds at 5000 feet & 7000 feet; therefore, much of the activity would have been hidden behind cloud, reports of 100 plus bandits in the immediate vicinity I would consider to be exaggerated. One question that could be asked is if a Messerschmitt Bf109 was engaged in conflict with an enemy plane Why didn't the pilot engage his cannons his most effective armament giving him a better opportunity to destroy his victim? There were no reports of cannon fire but there were reports of a pilot going to his death & also baling out. However stories of an aeroplane crashing in flames proved embellished as during the excavation of P3179 in 1996 none of the fuselage or engine were found to be bearing the hallmarks of fire damage, only the tail section & some of the wooden formers had burn marks, these would have burnt in the explosion on impact when the petrol tanks ruptured. Many letters received since the excavation were published in the Local & National Press together with Television had to be analysed, were they all mistaken identity, tricks of the mind, or true fact. We will try & determine what really did happen on that fatal day. At this point let's look at the true findings. We have evidence from perhaps the only person knowledgeable of what happened. **Squadron leader Badger** as C/O & leader of six Hurricanes of 'B' flight he recorded in the station log.

Intercepting 30 plus enemy aircraft he wrote, "*We sighted an enemy plane & rolled over to engage it Sgt Noble fell away & another plane came & took his place. He did not rejoin us & crashed. It is possible that a German gunner, may have fired a short burst at Sgt Nobles plane with devastating consequences*". Badger continues to explain, they had attacked a Junkers 88 in line astern formation. A favoured manoeuvre from cloud cover. Squadron Leader Badger's report also mentions negative German fighter cover. So what did the people on the ground observe? They would have seen Hurricanes line astern attacking the Junkers 88 & Sgt Noble falling away. As he did so the next Hurricane in line would move up to fill the space in the formation & may have appeared as though it was an attacking Me 109. A simple misinterpretation of what one observed during the raging battle. A misinterpretation that had been made many times previously, even pilots filling out combat reports were not immune to inaccuracy. If one was to observe a Messerschmitt Bf109 on the ground against a Hurricane it would not be difficult to tell them apart, but in the air & in the distance it would be very difficult, as other aircraft would also be weaving about the sky. Even British Ack Ack gunners were known to shoot at returning RAF fighters & during 'air' to 'air 'combat British planes had been known to open fire on one another, again mistaken identity.

Dennis Noble had been killed instantly or severely wounded as his Hurricane fell to earth reaching speeds of 400 mph, possibly at full throttle. If a German gunner had targeted his Hurricane, Dennis would have been lucky to escape at such close range. We have to understand that German gunners were armed with 7.92 mm machine guns & were anything but amateurs at gunnery, many had been involved in the attacks on the Low Countries & Poland, & therefore were relatively battle hardened. Only a few short bursts fired into a cockpit would be required to immobilize the pilot. Dennis fresh out of training had been fortunate up to now, with luck on his side over the past weeks.

At least three bullets entered the cockpit passing through Dennis's body finishing up in his parachute pack. No bullet holes were discovered in the pilots seat indicating that rounds of fired ammunition entered through the canopy from above possibly as he banked his machine behind the German bomber, but in front of its guns. During the last few seconds P3179 appeared to travel vertically from about 7000 feet hitting the ground at 11-58hrs. However the excavation showed the angle was more likely to have been 60-65 degrees, as the wing had clipped the gabled roof of 59 Woodhouse Road slightly turning the aircraft to port before its entry into the pavement, this would have happened in Mille-seconds. The Rolls-Royce Merlin traveled to a depth of 16 feet severing Gas & Water mains, the cockpit was discovered 6 to 8 feet south of the engine. Impact caused the petrol tanks to erupt in a ball of flame sending burning fuel up into apartments on the second floor of Portland Gate residential complex built in the 1930s. Occupants were seen throwing furniture & carpets over the balcony & into the street below. Flames had left a black scorch mark along the east-facing wall of the building that remained visible for years afterwards. One reason for this was that paints manufactured during this period were mainly water-based products such as white wash; this would not bond over the oily black stain. It was not until modern paints venture onto the market that it was finally covered. Wreckage was mostly confined around the crater with the entire fuselage under ground after smashing its way through concrete paving slabs before coming to an abrupt halt 16 feet below. Among the first components to be ripped off would have been the three wooden propeller blades followed by panels, Radiator & the top section of the Hurricanes fuselage. The wings broke off on impact remaining on the surface whereby the tail remained protruding from the crater with the wooden formers burnt beyond recognition. We can only hope that this devoted Baptist had offered a final prayer before

meeting his doom. Finally one comment from an eyewitness reported the pilot was fighting to gain control appearing to aim his stricken machine towards allotments at the top of Woodhouse Road, a course of that action would have avoided hitting houses. The speed involved as the Hurricane plummeted would have made it difficult if not impossible to see the movements of the pilot in detail.
However as the holder of a Private Pilots License myself & if faced with an emergency situation 'touch wood it does not come to that' the choice of hitting soft ground would be ones natural reaction, but whatever peoples sentiments were in 1940 I believe that Sgt Noble did everything that a dying man could do. He may have saved lives but this is pure speculation & cannot be proven, hostile times frequently play tricks with ones mind.

PORTLAND GATE
Where burning fuel entered apartments setting alight furniture

Crash site of Hurricane P3179 taken a few hours afterwards. The Taxi top left of picture was on hire from Higgins taxis Hove to the Co-operative funeral directors as a hearse due to the shortage of vehicles.

Sgt Dennis Nobles Grave in Retford Cemetery

Sgt DENNIS NOBLE remembered on the War Memorial in Retford Nottinghamshire.

WINGS OF A FALLEN ANGEL.

Fifty-six years has passed since Sgt Dennis Noble's death. Generations have learned about the plane crash in Woodhouse Road, Hove & the death of a British Airman who was recovered & laid to Rest in his home town during the Battle of Britain 1940. It was not until 1996 during the excavation of his Hurricane P3179 by Keith Arnold (Author) & **Southern Counties Aviation Club** that they made the grim discovery of human remains still in the wreckage. Questions immediately requiring answers were, ' If Sgt Noble had been buried in Retford with a known grave. 'How' or 'Why' was he still in the cockpit of his Hurricane?

To answer these questions we must first look at the facts surrounding the 30th August 1940 & try to understand circumstances prevailing just as the Battle of Britain reached its peak, apart from bombs dropping on coastal towns there were also planes falling from a battle torn sky, both British & German alike. This meant that salvage & repair crews were being stretched to the limit, working non-stop filling in bomb craters, shoring damaged buildings & of course clearing away the debris of crashed aircraft, one such machine being Dennis Noble's. Just after noon on the 30th August 1940 RAF appointed salvage crews & Civil Defence teams arrived at the scene, they discovered that apart from the obvious surface wreckage gas & water mains had been fractured, a scene that almost resembled the same site in 1996. Clearing the wreckage from around the hole they proceeded to repair the main services, a job that must be carried out with haste, as one would not know when or where, the next point of call would arise. It was war & salvage teams could ill afford to take time perfecting the job. Tools were basic only spades & forks, shovels picks & the odd crowbar. The luxury of hydraulic machines was not even thought of, at least to the extent of today's civil engineering equipment. Working against time they isolated all they could find of Dennis Noble & according to MOD records completed by the salvage team, indicated they had removed all of Dennis's remains.

Pulling at the wreckage with their bare hands was about all they could achieve as it was buried too deep. An important decision had to be made could anything be recovered from a crash of this enormity & for what purpose would it serve. As time was of importance to the salvage crews, bombers maybe overhead at any minute & the whole scenario repeated. Personnel & equipment might be required to rescue wounded people from a bombed out dwelling any minute so the dead could be left to rest. One wing was leant against the sidewall of Portland Gate flats & wreckage was stacked in a mangled heap on the corner of Woodhouse Road awaiting collection & guarded to stop souvenir hunters. People gathered to observe, lining Portland Road behind a roped off area just as they did again during the recovery in 1996. The corner fence of No 59 was destroyed, as was the front gable to the roof, but remarkably the front door of the house only twenty feet to the right of the impact hole suffered no major damage. The blast from the impact & fuel from the plane's tanks was blown away from the house causing no further damage. By now Sgt Noble's remains were on their way to Retford for burial. It was presumed the coffin contained a complete body & there was no reason to think otherwise. But alas this proved to be wrong never did the RAF or the MOD think that one of their pilots remained at the crash-site or it would have been declared a War Grave. **Saturday 31 August 1940** for Harry & Annie Noble was the day they had feared, a telegram from the Air Ministry arrived informing them of their son's death, plainly stating 'Killed in Action' very brief with no content describing 'how or when', a telegram similar to thousands received throughout the war.

Wednesday 4 September 1940 the Union flag draped over Dennis's coffin with four bearers proudly carrying the coffin into the Baptist Church where he had frequently attended services during his life at Hallcroft Road Retford. However mourners could not help noticing that one end of the coffin seemed heavier by the way the bearers carried it, also the angle of the coffin as it was lowered gracefully into the grave. Had something moved?

What could be an explanation for the distinctive tilt & extra strain on the shoulders of the coffin bearers? Research illustrates that during war & even in today's society requirements for coffins to be brought to the right respective weight for burial are sometimes required. It has been known to place sand bags or even sacks of potatoes in to a coffin due to the lack of human remains discovered at scenes of horrific accidents due to the forces of severe impact which can pulverise the human body causing only fragments to be found. This proved to be the case concerning Dennis Noble in 1940; it allowed relatives to mourn at the graveside of a departed loved one.

The cortege left the Baptist church after a short service, to Mendelssohn's O Rest in the Lord played on the organ. Slowly the procession made their way to the cemetery, a grave situated along the Chesterfield Canal winding its way through the town of Retford. On the request of Dennis's mother the grave was to be marked with a black Marble surround & not the normal Military headstone issued, rifles fired a volley of shots that echoed over the cemetery, a bugle played the Last Post ending the funeral that no-one would ever have thought would happen again fifty six years later.

13th November 1996 will stand out in my mind for a long time to come, a telephone call from the Sussex Coroner inviting my wife June & myself, Keith Arnold (Author) to pay our respects to & see the remains of Sgt Dennis Noble at the Brighton Mortuary, we had not for one minute realised that laying before us was almost a complete skeleton with some of the torso relatively intact. The coroner explained to us that the pieces missing would have not survived the impact & would have decayed, fibrous bones such as in the hands & feet would most certainly have been amongst the first to deteriorate.

So just what did they bury in 1940, well the answer to that is very little if any thing at all, because what I saw was approximately 80% of Sgt Dennis Noble.

Following more research into the matter of legal requirements

I discovered that before a corpse can be certified & linked to a name & proof of identity must be established beyond doubt. However it seems that if an entire corpse cannot be found & seven pounds of fleshy tissue perhaps ones leg, or if only a small fragment of Skull or vertebrae is found, life cannot be sustained & providing another form of identification is related then that is all the requirements need for burial.
This is why Sgt Noble & perhaps other pilots & crews have been left still in the wreckage of their machines only to be discovered when Archaeology or building development takes place. No-one during 1940 would have given thought to the fact that sites such as these would be re-opened years later & will most likely continue to periodically.
16th –17th November 1996 During the process of cleaning & under the supervision of the RAF we found more human remains entangled in the twisted fragments of wreckage. Promptly they were taken to Brighton Mortuary & placed in their respective location.

18th December 1996 was the date set for the Inquest as the law has to be satisfied before burial can be authorised Brighton Coroner **Dr Donald Gooding** presided his very last Inquest before his retirement. Wearing full robes as a mark of respect, the Court heard of the telegram sent to Dennis Noble's parents by Squadron Leader Badger & his report of the incident in 1940. Reverend **Tony Martlew** gave his report of the moments leading up to the crash as an eyewitness the verdict was given as Death by Enemy Action, Dr Gooding paid tribute in recognition of what Dennis Noble had achieved & to the debt we all owe him & pilots of the period. Putting Dennis's life into perspective, he said.
"The Battle was fought by very young men & boy's in their teens or early twenties, Winston Churchill spoke of them as The Few'& it was a tribute to him that we hold this Inquest. It appears quite possible Dennis died due to machine gun fire from an enemy bomber. These days we are regaled by talk of heroes,

Really I don't know what people are talking about, their heroes get large sums of money for kicking a soggy lump of leather about, these are just one type of today's so called heroes. "They are not true heroes, Dennis Noble was a Hero".
The Ministry of Defence was given the task of making arrangements for the second funeral, this was placed in the capable hands of 51 Squadron based at Waddington. You may ask why not 43-squadron, well the system requires that a burial must be organised by the nearest RAF establishment to the hometown of the deceased. In this instance, it was either Waddington or the training base at Cranwell. No one gets two military funerals therefore Dennis Noble could be no exception to the rules'. Arrangements made were of high quality except that no rifle volley would be fired. The C/O of 43 Squadron also a resident of Retford was to perform a Fly Past as a squadron salute, but as the funeral was set for **22 January 1997** the weather would dictate if a fly past was possible, alas fog persisted throughout the Midlands all day therefore the flypast was cancelled. The difference with a full military funeral & one with honours is that there are no church proceedings, only prayers at the graveside. Draped with the Union Flag & Sergeants Hat resting on top. Six Sergeants of equal rank withdrew his coffin from the hearse. After a journey that carried him for the last time through the streets of his hometown, the Reverend **Martin Loveless,** Chaplain of 51 squadron started the service with a short address praising the sacrifice Sgt Noble had made towards his Countries freedom. Then a prayer & Psalm were said .At the committal Reverend Loveless recited the touching poem 'High Flight' written by P/O J.G Magee Jnr, the act of remembrance was said during the lowering of the coffin by the Reverend **John Watts** also an eyewitness to the crash. In his words "On the morning of the 30 August 1940 while walking along the sea front at Hove my thoughts were, how could anyone survive that sort of impact" I heard no more of this incident as my family moved to Coventry. As years rolled by my thoughts often Returned to that young man, I neither knew his name or age but it

continued to haunt my memory. In 1986, a friend loaned me a book with the number of the Hurricane P3179 & the pilot's name. The mystery was solved, a few more years went by without the opportunity to visit his grave then as I grew older a startling event occurred. I remember preparing for Mass on Remembrance Sunday November 10th 1996, when I noticed that some one had placed three wooden crosses with in a display of wreathes & a book of war poems, I thought it a pity that the crosses had not been dedicated to a specific person, I wrote the names of my uncle & cousin both killed in action & on the last cross the name Dennis Noble flashed into my consciousness so I wrote his name upon it & placed it back into the display. At the end of Mass I went home for breakfast before returning to Church for the main Service. Whilst eating my breakfast I asked my wife if there was anything of interest on the news' No' she replied, Oh except they have recovered the body of an airman from a road in Hove, Brighton. On hearing the name I almost choked on my cup of tea, it seemed astonishing that only an hour ago I had placed his name on the wooden cross. Naturally the thought entered my mind, is he buried in Retford! I later read of the excavation & how Sgt Noble had been discovered. The next development was when my brother in law telephoned to say that a military Funeral had been planned. On receiving this information I contacted Reverend Loveless & he kindly invited me to attend & say the Act of Remembrance at the service. I shall remember this young man for the rest of my life. May he through God's Tender Love & Mercy Rest in Peace".
After the internment I was fortunate enough to meet some of Dennis Nobles family & friends, many had not met for years. A family dispersed over the four corners of the country. Remaining in Retford are his cousin **Ethyl Knight** & **Mrs D Scott.** Unfortunately, Dennis's Brother John could not attend as illness made it impossible for him to travel. John passed away a few months later with the knowledge that his brother had been returned home. What I will never forget were the tears of sorrow the six sergeant coffin bearers expressed, as they paid a last salute to a

'Fallen Angel'.
This letter from the Reverend **H.T Mogridge** to Harry & Annie Noble perhaps sums up the end of this chapter.

Aldrington Rectory, Hove.

December 20th 1940
Dear Mrs Noble

"Thank you and your husband for your kind letter and for the photograph of your hero son. We shall treasure the letter very much and I propose to place it near the Roll of Honour in the church which contains the name of your son as he died in this parish and also the names of four of the boy's from this parish, who have given their lives in this war so far.

I am also sending you a copy of our year book for last year we have not got one for this year I am afraid owing to shortage of paper but this one contains a map of the parish and I have marked on it exactly where your son met his death. There is a vacant space not yet built on at the top of Woodhouse Road and Coleman Avenue and that is where the plane fell.

I am afraid that at Christmas time the loss of our gallant boy is bought home to us very much indeed and you may like to know that we shall be remembering Dennis at our Christmas Services.

May I wish you all as Happy a Christmas as is possible for you under the circumstances and express the hope that 1941 will bring us Victory & Peace

I am yours sincerely

H T Mogridge

The REVEREND H.T MOGRIDGE

Funeral of Sgt Noble in Retford, 1997.

YEILDS OF MOTHER EARTH.

During the 'Battle of Britain' raging air battles over the English countryside were perhaps best remembered by those who lived in the South, watching massed formations of German bombers cross the coast with British fighters on their heels, vapour trails weaving patterns across the sky as planes engaged in life or death manoeuvres. Several planes perished in the labyrinth of the fields, others sank into the English Channel, but in the case of Hurricane P3179 a residential street. As in recent years these objects of war have become a part of our heritage, with aviation enthusiasts establishing a relatively new pastime that has become known Aviation Archaeology, the pilots of these machines becoming heroes. As we all owe our freedom to them.

In many cases, history is being recorded & its remnants kept for future generations to learn of their Country's conflict. If relics or pieces of twisted metal as they sometimes appear to look were left to the elements & time, deterioration would dissolve all traces & some of our history of 1940 left in disarray. People all over Britain owe their freedom & existence to the pilots & ground crews of the Royal Air Force. Brave deeds & acts of heroism will be remembered forever through memoirs & documentation".

In recent years since the end of World War Two, recovery teams have dedicated their time recording truthful accounts of the air battles that raged over Britain. Memory & inaccurate documentation every now & then mystifies the activities that took place during the summer of 1940.

'Aviation recovery teams' consist of sincere individuals that have the highest regard & respect for those pilots that fought & died in their machines of war, for many of us they are our 'heroes' of a heroic period. Aviation Archaeology is an operation approached with the highest regard for pilots & crews without forgetting their families. Probably the most famous hunting grounds for the archaeologist to roam are the fields of Kent & Sussex where many aircraft types fell to the guns of their opponents, in some areas

There are crash sites, only a few hundred yards apart, almost unbelievable that fields so close together can surrender historical artefacts in pristine condition. It is also true that if no attempt is made to recover the twisted remains of these war machines, decay & corrosion over the next century will most certainly eradicate all traces of history, & evidence of what actually happened will be lost forever.

The Battle of Britain in particular was unique & probably the most decisive battle Britain has had to face. As we know, life would have been very different if the boot had been on the other foot, with the German Army walking up to Westminster with Hitler in full control. An invasion of our coast would have been inevitable had the RAF not succeeded in holding back the Luftwaffe. Invasion barges were only twenty-two miles across the channel from Dover, waiting for the command to load with front line troops. Operation Sea Lion was to be carried out 17th September 1940; landing areas had already been designated from Folkestone to St Leonard's, Bexhill to Eastbourne & Beachy Head to Brighton. Airborne landings along the Royal Military Canal in Kent & the South Downs behind Brighton. Nine Wermacht divisions were assembled for the assault, Junkers Ju 87s were to act as artillery during the early part of the attack poised at bases in Pas de Calais & around Baie de la Siene, all that was needed was air superiority.

After the war eyewitness, accounts of air battles & crash sites brought a new beginning, 'Aviation Archaeology' of a chivalrous nature; but it was not until the sixties that this sort of activity really took a grasp. During the war children were often at the scene of a crash before salvage crews could arrive & pieces of plane were taken home as a spontaneous sentimental reward. Then during the 1970s groups of hunters started to form, many were teams from museums now setting standards to preserve the treasures discovered. The **Kent Battle of Britain Museum**, Hawkinge. **Brenzett** on the Romney Marsh in Kent & **Tangmere Aviation Museum**, Sussex. Private collections started to develop including the collection of Keith Arnold (Author). Getting up on a Saturday morning spade in hand then off to visit a crash site that one had previously researched, to find what treasures the earth would yield. For the duration of the 1960-70s a Ministry of Defence licence was not required & in fact all that was needed was landowners permission most of whom were very thoughtful & excited. It was known to dig one site in the morning & another in the afternoon, however this sort of activity could not continue at its present rate with more aircraft being uncovered locating new sites became difficult. Occasionally a pilot or crewmember would be found in the wreckage although this was rare & usually purely by accident, as incorrect combat reports by pilots sometimes produced inaccurate positions of aircraft destroyed. A number of aeroplanes damaged in combat did not make it home finishing up in fields or the English channel without being reported until much later when their exact locations were reported incorrectly. After many digs public outcry into the knowledgeable digging of some 'known to be war graves' made it necessary for the Government to act & introduce a special licence enforced by the MOD, for the practice of military excavations. However this type of licence was not enforced until the 1980s. One has to prove that pilots or crews are not still in the aircraft before digging takes place, applications also require written permissions & map references to within 100 metres, one must conform to the licence at all times or fines of three figures can be imposed. Now that a new Millennium is upon us aviation teams still carry on with excavations but now with a much finer approach. There are still a number of sites not yet divulged & there will undoubtedly be other pilots or crews un-earthed at times, accidentally or maybe recovered by the RAF upon the request of relatives to the MOD.

This is the story of one excavation that took place under the guidance of the MOD licence 'not in an open field or in woodland but below a residential street in the bustling seaside resort of Brighton & Hove, Hawker Hurricane P3179, of 43 squadron based at Tangmere took off soon after 11.20hrs Friday 30th August 1940 to intercept incoming German raiders crossing the coast at Hove. A British fighter aeroplane piloted by Sgt Dennis Noble who had only joined the squadron 27 days earlier plunged into the Eastern pavement of Woodhouse Road Hove, within a millionths of a second both Sgt Noble & his Hurricane disappeared below ground, leaving a crater behind only a few feet from No 59 & the vacant piece of land, once allotments adjacent to Portland Road. As the plane smashed its way through the granite paving slabs disintegrating as it ploughed into the earth, the petrol tanks exploded sending petrol into adjacent flats. When Civil Defence teams & Army personnel arrived it was apparent to them that the pilot could not have survived. They set about removing what meagre remains of him they could find on the surface & accessible around the hole, then moving onto the wreckage, clearing it away & neatly stacking it on the North East corner of Woodhouse Road for the RAF salvage team to transport later. After completing major repairs to the gas & water mains, the crater was in filled & the site forgotten. There are those with hindsight that have remembered where one of the 'Few' died, it is a fact that on the 50th Anniversary 1990 of his death only one person showed tangible remembrance by providing a spray of red, white & blue flowers, also placing a notice in the local evening paper. Critics of the subsequent excavation of P3179 obviously had short memories. However, those who did not forget included members of **Southern Counties Aviation Club**. During the 1960s a home for the elderly was built on the waste ground that had once been the allotments close to the crash site & after a number of years became outdated & had to make way for a new complex of residential apartments to be built by **Chichester Diocesan Housing Association**. Before the old nursing home was finally demolished a story materialised from a few of the nurses that had worked there 'perhaps one could say this story is myth or convincingly true nevertheless, it remains the narrative account of sincere individuals.

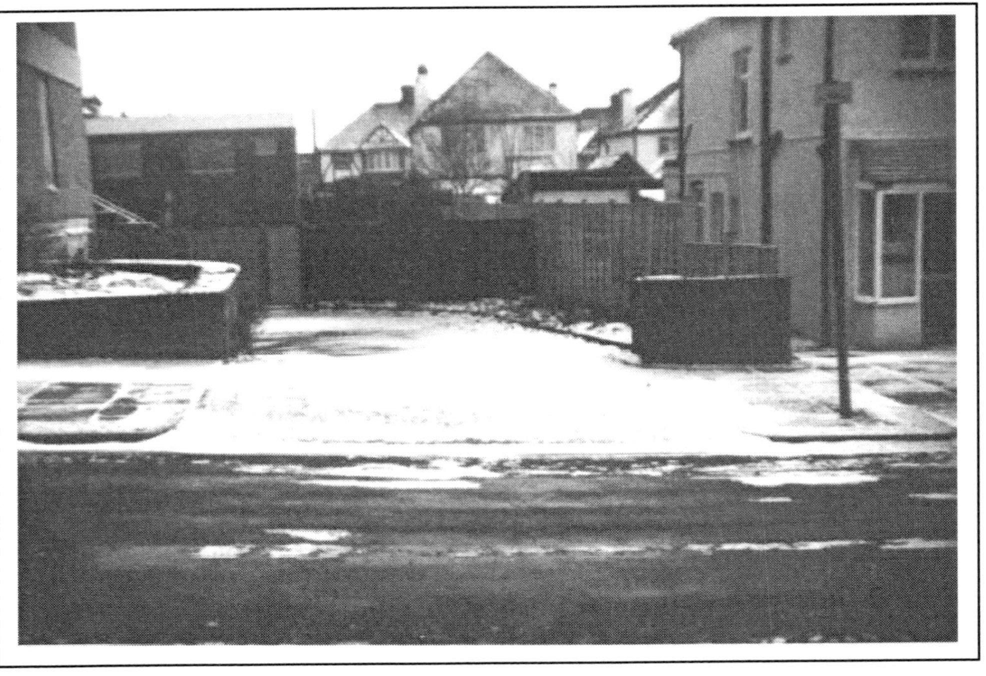

Crash-site 1996 before the excavation took place

TOP. *Woodhouse Road Crash site 30th August 1940.*
BELOW*, Crash site in 1995 before the excavation of Hurricane P3179. X marks the centre of the crater, the wreckage still remains buried 16 feet below the pavement.*

A tale that has been told to family & friends many times, but was convincing enough to those concerned. 'One elderly resident at the home used to catch sight of a ghostly figure dressed in 1940s pilots flying attire sitting on her bed late at night, this happened quite often & as this lady described gave lasting comfort, also the same figure had been seen in the corridors by various Nurses at different times throughout the nights.
Throughout the demolition of the old nursing home work was plagued with misfortune, one worker fell down a flight of stairs & was seriously injured, was he startled? Misfortune also continued during the early stages of construction of the new flats, with two more accidents one a carpenter severing a hand & yet another worker falling, there were many other smaller problems such as a strike by brick layers, work was delayed many times, co-incidence who knows but one thing is for sure as soon as Sgt Noble had been discovered the building site did not suffer again in fact everything went according to plan. I will leave these observations open for contemplation.

Getting back to the job at hand making plans for the recovery of P3179 is something that needed careful organisation. One cannot drive up with a mechanical digger & a group of volunteers & calmly start digging up the road; firstly, you must approach the relevant authorities & landowners. Then a survey must be carried out to define the exact area to be unearthed, an excavation of this magnitude & to a depth of five to seven metres is a major undertaking. Even if successful the site will subsequently have to be restored to its original status, this sort of operation can be costly & volunteers would be greatly appreciated. On a site such as Woodhouse Road no end of problems could arise, each one would have to be tackled with professionalism. When an excavation takes place in a field, there is a good chance of nothing going wrong but on an urban site, even access becomes an obstacle. Errors can only be minimised through planning because underneath the pavement lay not only aircraft wreckage but gas, water, electric &

telephone services. A very expensive fibre optic British Telecom cable ran directly through the centre of the hole. These all had to be traced & accurately plotted before any work could be undertaken, metal detectors aided this task making various sweeps of the pavement on both sides of the road. Drains had to be located using charts, we also needed to access materials most likely to be used in the event of an emergency perhaps a fractured gas or water pipe. We considered digging a slit trench along the pavement to help establish what lay beneath, but decided to wait for one final test result & another possible source to locate the exact spot, considering any additional damage caused to the pavement, the more time & cost it will take to restore. One treasured source & specific proof was a photograph taken a few hours after the crash then placed into the Brighton Herald Newspaper under the caption "Death of a Hun" Studying the picture closely we worked out the location by tracing the line of fence & working out measurements of its entire length to the relevant point of entry. During our next visit to the crash-site, Colin Lee bought along a more powerful metal detector to verify the amount of wreckage lying below & at what depth. Readings showed significant objects well under ground, so we marked the circumference of the point of entry on the pavement with chalk, it was not until that moment we realised just how lucky the people living at number 59 had been in 1940, because the aperture of the hole marked was only 20ft from the front door of the house.

The next task was to apply to the MOD for a licence & to organise necessary equipment etc, this turned out to be a bigger task than expected, as permission from the Council would be required. Soon it became apparent that we were facing difficulties with the paper work of bureaucracy. We needed to acquire an accredited supervisor somebody qualified in highway engineering & we discovered there were only four qualified persons in Sussex, & none available from the council. Eventually however BT loaned us the expertise of **Tony Diamond.** One minute we could not locate a supervisor then suddenly we had two when **Colin Southhouse** from Hailsham Construction Company came to assist. Winter was just around the corner & the target date set was 8th November 1996. We calculated three days would be required to complete the task with possibly a further two days cleaning the site up, apart from the necessary team & machinery, the responsibility of Health & Safety also security of the site had to be planned. Media coverage concerning the project could cause problems with enlarged numbers of the public in attendance, their safety had to be supreme before all else. We informed the police who kept a watchful eye, & 176 Squadron ATC (*Air Training Corps*) provided escort to members of the public moving about the site. There was no shortage of volunteers to join the team, excavating a war time aeroplane does not happen very often & bought a keen interest from many individuals, It was essential that each stage of the recovery was recorded fully & we decided that two photographers would be required. One was the excellent amateur **Martin Reilly,** the other **Peter Watson** from Brighton University studying his A levels in the subject. Browns kindly loaned us the use of earth moving machines & lorries to dispose of unwanted soil, so it was all systems 'Go'. Finally, on 5th November 1996 most of the team met at my house, at that time in Handcross, West Sussex, ready to attempt an early start. On our arrival at the site we coned off the immediate area & proceeded to remove the front gate brick wall of Number 59, under the watchful eye of Mr **Paul Kendal** owner of the property promptly scratching his head as his garden began to resemble a building site. 10am & our first predicament arose; the safety fence & signs had not yet arrived. Meanwhile; we continued, removing the first paving slabs our perseverance began to pay off, just 18inches below the pavement our first discoveries were made. Small fragments of alloy accompanied by a cluster of 303 rounds still in the clip, then one of the propeller stubs with fragments of the wooden blade attached. Could it be that other items discovered would be in such perfect order? Adrenaline started to flow through one's veins rapidly as the excitement of what lay below undisturbed for

Fifty-six years would soon be brought to the surface. The first of the earth moving machines arrived in the capable hands of **John Milham** & shortly afterwards came the fencing.

Very soon, a large mound of earth ascended to the front window leaving Mr Kendal's lounge, creating the impression from inside that one was under ground.

Before this pile could be removed the soil had to be checked, a task taken on by **Tony Martlew** & my twelve year old son **Simon Arnold**, they turned over each of the heavy clods of earth to reveal small items of the Hurricane left behind after the first analysis. The main site hole had reached 8 feet & wooden shoring was needed before one could work safely, the question was that the line of wreckage was not going down vertically, the angle started following a more Northerly direction at about 45 degrees, this angle would destroy any chance of fixing wooden shoring to the sides of the hole. We decided that if the heavy clay sub-soil proved stable & solid we could continue but only with one person working in the hole at any one time & another within reach in case an emergency arose. Suddenly a distinct aroma of fuel hovered about the site. Deciding that we must have discovered trapped petrol from the Hurricanes 28 gallon reserve tank, we scooped up as much of this cocktail as we could into containers for later disposal.

At least Dennis Noble had been spared the torture of an inferno as the Hurricane plunged earthwards many pilots were burned or disfigured after suffering an exploding fuel tank ending up as one of **Sir Archibald McIndoe's** Guinea Pigs in the famous East Grinstead Burns hospital, along side famous names such as **P/O Tom Cleave** & **P/O P. H. V Wells** of 249 Squadron & many others who owe their looks & new found confidence to this pioneering surgeon, able to face the outside world after severe disfigurements. He gave them just that.

The main services such as the gas & water supplies had to be kept maintained at all time, therefore we could ill afford any damage

to the pipes that hung suspended over the hole. One was a BT fibre optic cable of astronomical cost, we did not wish to cause damage to this piece of modern technology. Luckily, something the salvage crews in 1940 did not have to contend with. These pipes were only 3 feet apart & with the excavator arm & bucket between them the gap decreased to inches, one slight mishap & danger would be upon us, the best way forward was for the person in the hole to give hand signals to another on the surface relaying them to the machine operator, risky but effective.
Night fell upon us quickly so we decided to stop work for the day & set about cleaning up the site. Suddenly in the reflection of the arc lights, we saw what appeared to be material, upon further investigation we discovered it was Dennis Noble's parachute still with the pack attached. Wet & covered in mud we unfolded it revealing a perfect conditioned silk (Irvin) parachute still bearing the date of manufacture (July 1940), certainly a prized possession that would have made many silk ladies undergarments if discovered in 1940. Parachutes fetched a good price on the black market & many pilots' parachutes finished up this way.

Further examination provided us with grimmer evidence as to what lay ahead. We discovered two bullet holes with bloodstain this gave us something else to consider for the next day.
Just with in our grasp was the oxygen bottle, removing this meant that we had reached the cockpit for sure as it is situated just be hind the pilots seat of a Hurricane. Once again, it was immaculate. The stencilled writing was legible just as though one had placed it there the day before, appearing as though time had not been evident. Finally two of the team volunteered to sleep in their cars overnight acting as night watchmen & hospitality soon rendered the task much easier when local residents provided refreshments & the use of household facilities. Early next morning
9th November 1996 we set about removing the large pile of earth in front of Number 59, the large excavator arrived, allowing us to dig deeper & bucketfuls of wreckage were soon hoisted to the top.

All types of twisted steel & components from the Hurricane surfaced. This is modern archaeology at its best, something that is normally associated with Roman ruins or another period in history. Requiring protection from the elements were pieces of fabric still bearing the RAF painted roundel, the gun sight, instruments & many other artefacts all in amazing condition, then everything was photographed & documented before being placed into containers for transportation.

As it was Saturday the local radio had been broadcasting details of what was happening in Woodhouse Road & bystanders increased gradually a constant assembly of around 50-60 people. At approximately 11.00 hrs the nature of the operation changed dramatically. We had reached the cockpit area, & the discovery of human remains, this brought a sort of respectful silence as word spread around the site, a prompt decision was made in the order of priority of what to do next! Sgt Dennis Noble was by chance about to be repatriated to the land & the people he loved & died defending, & as the MOD licence holder it fell upon myself (Author) to take immediate action concerning this tragic discovery. The licence issued by the MOD prescribes a set procedure of the requirements one must enforce, all excavation ceased forthwith & non-essential personnel were ordered to leave the immediate area. The Ministry of Defence, Police & Coroner were informed & the site vacated.

Uncovering what appears to be a war grave happens occasionally during projects such as this & will happen from time to time. The South of England still hold s the key to many missing war planes of various nationalities & this unfortunate discovery of one of England's Few will most likely not be the last. Stress & pressure had been placed upon the recovery crews during wartime, where often they would have to mingle between crash-sites, so the complete recovery of human remains was given low priority. The emphasis in 1940 was on defence & protection of the living or wounded not on the entombed dead.

In the case of Dennis Noble the possibility of invasion forces landing within a fortnight on beaches barely ½ mile away to the south, manpower could not be used for a meticulous search for human remains of a pilot whose aeroplane had dived at 400 mph from 7000 feet into the earth. Thankfully in today's world there are no such considerations.

We took prudent steps to ensure that Dennis should receive in 1996 the dues that the severity of war had denied him in 1940. The first procedure was to erect plastic sheeting around the site fence, to shield our discovery from prying eyes & cameras especially the latter for the behaviour of a minority of the press was shameful. Well-equipped photographers from national & local newspapers arrived as soon as word leaked out. A minority acted in a way that we all felt appalling, some tried to take pictures below the plastic sheet shielding the site, even climbing onto balconies of the overlooking flats of Portland Gate, others tried to bribe residents offering money £25-£100 was the going rate to use an overlooking bedroom window to take their photographs, only to be met by blunt refusals & suggestions that they show respect for a dead hero. (This was true gutter press) Many of the reporters were by contrast deeply moved.

The group did its best to reward those patient enough to wait singling them out for information & photographic opportunities once circumstances permitted, nevertheless it is a story that will find a place in ones heart.

It did not take the police long to arrive closely followed by the Coroner. I explained the terms of the licence to them & waited for a decision as to the task of removing Sgt Noble, the Coroner decided that owing to the nature & planning that had gone into this recovery it would be best if the team acted under his jurisdiction as we would be best qualified for the job.

The hole was slowly filling with water & more wreckage required removing before we could get within reach of Sgt Noble. Up to now no one could officially identify who the pilot was, because we had not yet discovered anything to prove the identity of the plane.

Immense consideration was given to clearing the remains of Sgt Noble from the wreckage of P3179, even personal items such as his wallet, address book, & his prayer book. Nothing was left behind; other items discovered were his uniform, shoes & his cap. Articles of clothing brought home the fact that this really, once was a living person, his tie exposed just the way he had knotted it earlier that morning, also retrieved was his belt still buckled. Inside his wallet a 1/6d ticket for Chichester cinema, this could have been an evening out with a close friend, possibly 'Patchy pocket, a nickname given to a WAAF who has not yet been identified, but was seen to accompany him on various occasions with Dennis's long time friend **Ken Lowe** stationed with him at 6 OTU & later at Tangmere.

No cavity in the hole was left unchecked, when certain that all had been cleared & the Coroner was satisfied, we decided to allow reporters to photograph until the all clear was given to continue with the excavation. Some of the Newspapers were misleading expressing that we had discovered the pilot still dressed in his flying jacket & sitting at his controls, why such ludicrous statements were printed makes the mind boggle'! If the plane was being removed in thousands of pieces I am sure the human body could not withstand such forces.

Sgt Noble's uniform was taken to Hove police station where it was placed in a locker to dry; the police acknowledged they were honoured to give Dennis's possessions a final caring touch. Albatross Wings & Sgt stripes identified the remains found as a Sergeant pilot, but we still could not say officially this was definitely Sgt Noble. Positive proof of identity had to be established.

The crash site had been cordoned off with blue & white tape with police present, sightseers had by now increased four-fold after the news was released on television & local radio.

The coroner asked me to transport the funeral casket containing Dennis's remains to the Brighton Mortuary on completion of our days work, as there was a chance that we could find more remains.

Meanwhile, we were still extracting many parts of the Hurricane. The control column had been found still with the gun button set to fire, nostalgic thoughts entered our minds as we took it in turns to hold this piece of engineering, realising that the last person to touch this had been Dennis Noble. Earlier in the day, I had wondered what would be the next problem to arise. This thought was rapidly becoming nightmarish, the next problem being a small water pipe connecting Number 59 Woodhouse Road with the water supply, a sudden movement of the excavator arm sent water gushing everywhere. My brother **Trevor Arnold** jumped into action diverting the water into the gutter before attempting an emergency repair. Cold & wet, he eventually succeeded in stopping the gushing liquid. Good news awaited, the Rolls-Royce Merlin engine had been exposed, a marvellous sight to see, with the manufacturers name impressed on the rocker covers & in pristine condition apart from being damaged after the impact. One problem left was how to retrieve it from the depths of the muddy cavity'. It was wedged firmly into the wall of the hole & lodged underneath the edge of the roadway 15 feet down. Could it be brought to the surface as it was somewhat large measuring 4 feet across & 7 feet in length remembering we had only 3 feet between the pipes on the surface surely we would not have to leave this Merlin where it originally landed, with only photographs to recall it. There was only one way to find out. Carefully digging around it to make way for lifting chains, we then attempted to lift the engine from the suction of the clay, which was holding it back with tremendous power. Suddenly it broke into large pieces, damage sustained was to our advantage as now it would pass between the pipes, slowly each piece was lifted out onto the awaiting transport giving bystanders their first glimpse of the engine so many had seen falling earthwards in 1940. Buckets of water were tipped over the engine revealing its black factory paintwork as bright as the day it went into the ground. It was possible to catch engine oil draining from various parts of the casing still as clean as the day engine fitters poured it into the oil tank at Tangmere airfield.

As dusk fell the site became peaceful & we placed the casket containing the remains of Sgt Noble into the Range Rover that was to haul the Hurricane wreckage back to a storage facility. We then waited for the police to escort us to the mortuary at a time pre-arranged with the Coroner.
I shall never forget this sentimental moment, as it was to be the last time Sgt Noble would travel with his Hurricane & somehow it seemed absolute. The legal obligation of the Coroner had been fulfilled, we could all now go home & rest, ready for the next day.

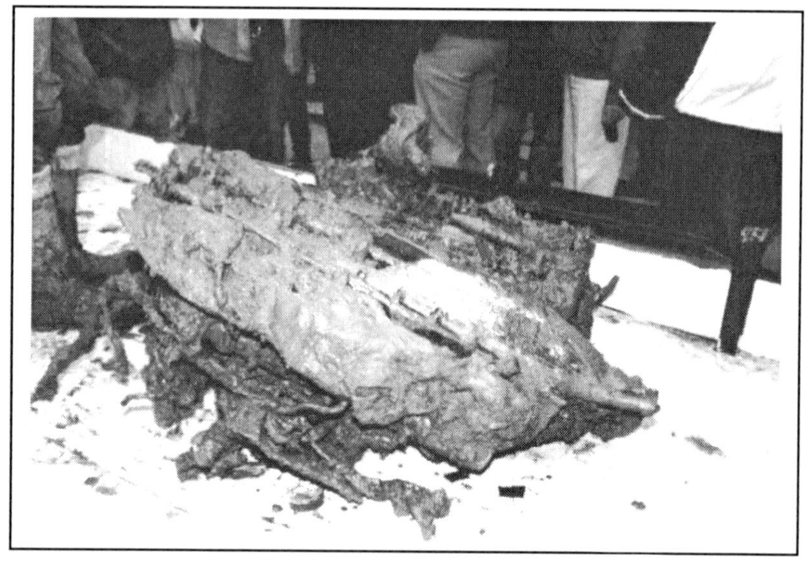

One of three large pieces of the engine,
Bearing the name ROLLS-ROYCE

Another bucketful of Hurricane wreckage surfaces

The Control Column is discovered after 56 years

Oxygen bottle surfaces

ATC view the crash site

Working into the night

Picture taken looking upwards from crash site

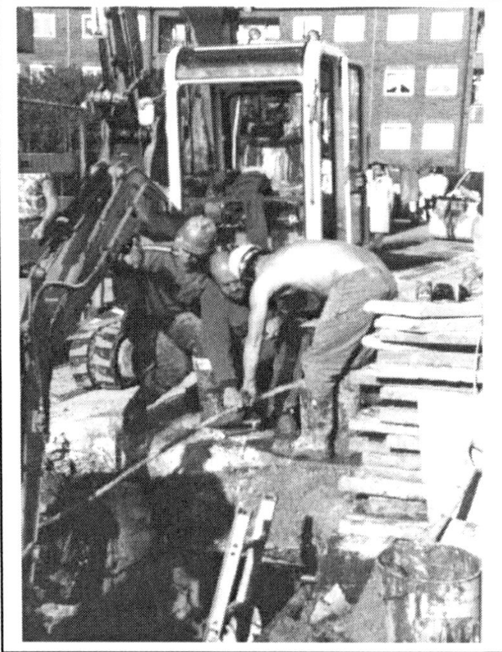

Making

Repairs to the

Fractured

Water Pipe.

Wreckage
Extracted from
The crash site.

(Please note)

Remains of
Pilots seat and
Other Cockpit
Remnants

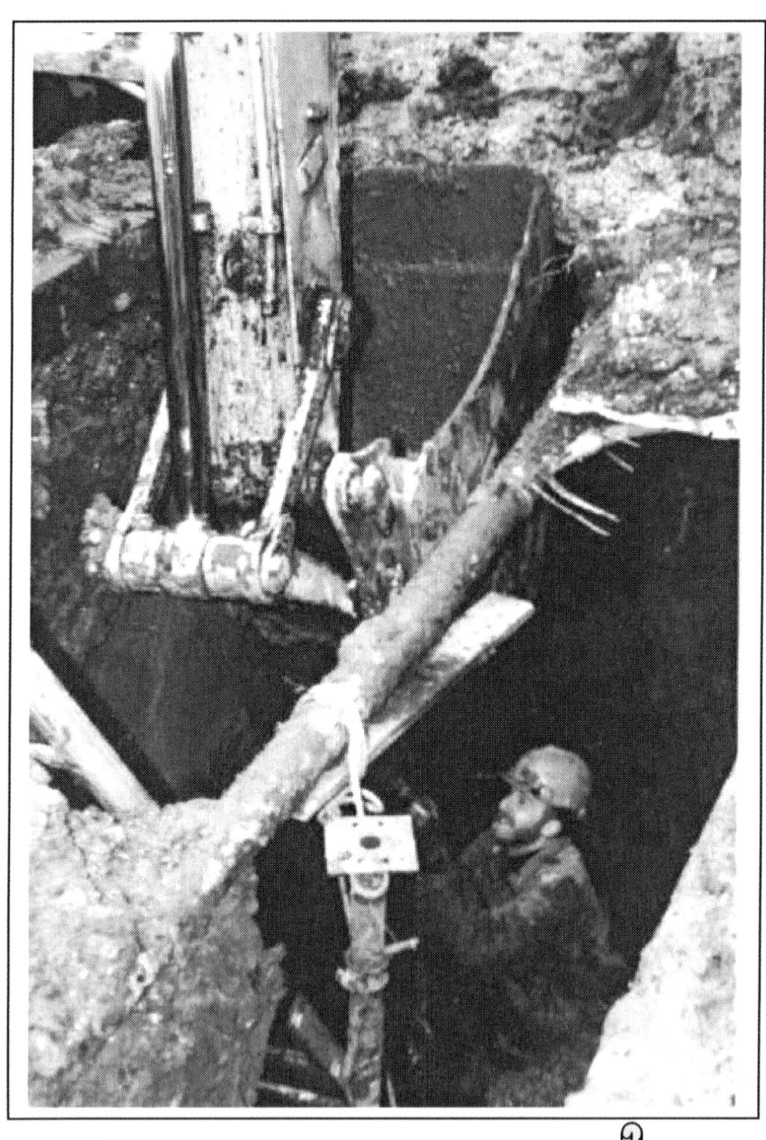

Working to within inches of Disaster Trying to Bring the Rolls-Royce Merlin Engine to the surface.

Team Member with
Top of Radio.

Keith Arnold Jnr with
Oxygen Gauge

Author Holding
Control Column

Gun sight Optic

Rolls-Royce Merlin engine recovered from crash-site in woodhouse road. Although badly damaged, its condition is excellent. When the engine oil escaped on impact it impregnated the soil forming an airtight seal this kept corrosion to a minimum.

Remembrance Day was celebrated on **Sunday 10th November 1996.** Therefore, we decided it would be appropriate to honour this brave airman, Sgt Dennis Noble before work continued. By lucky chance **Cyril Linter** along with his wife **Rose** who had kept us fed & watered, just happened to be Secretary of the Hove branch of the Royal Air Force Association. Several telephone calls & two hours later, a ceremony was arranged. British Legion & RAFA members would parade near the site, joined with 176 Squadron ATC Hove.

We had planned to take the Merlin engine back to the site so people to view the previous days discovery, but an unfortunate breakdown occurred & we had to settle for a few smaller items.

Just before the service started, we opened Sgt Nobles parachute placing it alongside the hole, with the control column, radio, & oxygen tank together with a bouquet of flowers that had been left on the excavator overnight. Rain overnight had created a pond & had to be pumped from the hole before the ceremony could take place. Meanwhile; members of the team searched the remaining mound of extracted earth & made another thorough check of the hole only to reveal more artefacts one being Sgt Noble's Parachute release buckle. After tidying up the site, we removed the sheeting from the security fence in order to let members of the public view the site for the first time& allowing photographs to be taken. By the end of our prayers, the hole was a mass of red poppies. Wreathes & sprays of flowers were left close by, increasing dramatically over the coming days.

10.45 am the North end of Woodhouse Road filled with bystanders waiting to pay homage to a pilot many had been unwittingly walking over since 1940. TV film crews arrived constantly. This service was very different to others taking place all over the Country. Our small ceremony was to honour a fallen hero discovered just 24 hours before. The Reverend **Tony Martlew** who as a boy witnessed the Hurricane's fatal dive took his place beside the crater just behind the parachute. 176 squadron ATC marched in from the junction of Portland Road and

Woodhouse Road followed by RAFA & British Legion Standards Then at 11.00hrs all those present stood for a two-minute silence. Reverend Tony Martlew presiding started the Service with prayers & read the poem "High flight" written by Canadian Pilot John Gillespie Magee killed in a collision over Lincolnshire 1941 aged 19. The service continued with the Lords Prayer & Sermon.
Afterwards many people were overcome by emotion whilst laying wreaths & wooden crosses, many placed their poppies in the hole. Something that will frequent my thoughts forever & will undoubtedly restore my faith in the media for a long time to come, was that one television film crew, professionally hardened to the aspects of News coverage, seeing pitiful sights whilst performing their duties had previously asked me for an interview, after the Service. I was completely surprised to see the interviewer in tears, & the cameraman also asked if he could wait until he had collected his thoughts.
Our simple Service had really bought home the accomplishment that Dennis Noble had died for. Approximately 100 people had been in attendance residents, passers by, members of the team & those that heard of our service via the radio many stayed behind for most of the morning & into the early afternoon.
Our next priority was to fill in the hole. Lorries containing crushed concrete arrived & commenced the tipping their loads all this concrete had to be compacted before we could close the site for the day.
Unforeseen at this time was the formalities & legal complications needing to be dealt with. On **Monday 11th November 1996** contact with the MOD proved rather complicated, as they wanted positive identification of the Hurricane & pilot so they dispatched from St Athens South Glamorgan, Warrant Officer **Tom Barton.** From the R.A.F crash recovery team. His first port of call was the crash-site, where he told me not to continue reinstating the site, as there might be a possibility that the RAF would want to reopen it. I explained that nothing of Hurricane P3179 remained in the hole & we had acted on behalf of the Coroner & that he was satisfied.

British Legion Standard Bearer and 176 Squadron ATC, below the balcony that was set alight after the crash in 1940.

TOP, *176 Squadron ATC Hove.*

BELOW, *Laying of wreathes, at the crash site 1996.*

Tom Barton filed his report soon followed by the reaction from the Ministry it was suggested that the wreckage should be transported to RAF Wittering for detailed examination by an RAF team. Luckily Tom intervened on our behalf & the MOD had second thoughts agreeing that our team was probably better equipped & more knowledgeable of the Hurricane than the RAF. After all they deal with modern aircraft rather than those of half a century ago. Heartened by this surprisingly sensible decision our group at once put to hand the closest possible search of the wreckage, determined to find the identification required. It was to be done under the watchful eye of **Taffy Simmonds** from St Athans RAF unit, who promptly arrived at my home on **15th November.** Over a few drinks at our local Social Club plans were made for an operation to clean as many parts of the Hurricane as we could, devising a wash bay was the easy bit, what appeared to be very basic turned out to be first class. Placing a wire mesh grill over an old trailer then with the parts laid out we could wash accumulated soil away, leaving them clean & the unwanted soil in the bottom of the trailer. Spreading a large plastic sheet out on the ground we emptied all the containers of remnants out, then we located what parts we thought would be fruitful & bear the numbers required, it was amazing to see for the first time just how much we had exposed, by chance the eighth piece we cleaned provided us with the number, at last we had solid proof that the part in question was an engine bearer with P3179 stamped into the metal. This number now confirmed the Hurricane & through records already gathered it could be linked to Sgt Dennis Noble of 43 Squadron along with dates & times. Our homemade wash bay continued in operation until every part had been washed. During this laundering we actually found three more parts bearing P3179 one a small fragment of alloy from the airframe, another was painted onto a fragment of plywood from the cockpit area, the third a piece of airframe structure. There was also a significant bonus for amongst the parts freed from the old Sussex clay was what seemed nothing at first but a ball of mud about the size of a football.

However; as the water jet demolished the outer shell we found to our amazement, that we had stumbled upon the pilots map box, inside & tightly packed were Sgt Nobles flying maps. Carefully extracting the folded maps, we laid them onto the nearest flat surface, this being the nearest available car bonnet, we then proceeded to unravel them whilst the pages remained wet as they could be separated easier. I took them into my house & carefully placed them on every available surface to dry, after about a week I placed the relevant pages in order, it turned out there were three maps perfectly readable, covering the South, South West, North East & fragments of North West England. They have since been framed with two displayed at Tangmere Aviation Museum.

We were all very thankful for the help that Taffy a true professional had given us over the four days of cleaning. It was decided that the engine was best left out to the elements until time was available to scrape away the clay & rain would keep the composite of mud & oil wet preventing it from drying out making the cleaning operation difficult. Exposed metal parts were sprayed with a mixture of oil & diesel, & everything else was packed away until we could continue with renovation work. Urgent work needed to be embarked upon reinstating Number 59, still bearing the hallmarks of a building site as we had left it by order of the RAF. Residents had been very supportive throughout the operation, therefore all they could hope for was the area would be returned to its original state. After many trips to the site throughout the coming weeks, everything was fully restored.

Over the next couple of years the bits & pieces had to be cleaned thoroughly & mounted for display this was done during our spare time. First on the agenda had to be the pilot's personal items found during the clarification procedure. Sgt Noble was blessed with a heavenly family & one such member was his Nephew befittingly named **Denis Noble junior.** We have become great friends over the past few years & have been successful in securing the personal effects of Sgt Noble for all to see. Items such as his nail file still in its leather case, part of a set that included

His wallet & address book also his prayer book all as matching leather set, exposed during the dig. Other items found during the restoration were his Sgt Stripes & Badge, an old penny piece, a farthing & half crown coins. Also fragments of his RAF tunic & shirt & one side of his goggles. These are proud reminders that he once was just an ordinary human being that gave his life for mankind.

During the recovery other personal items were found & subsequently handed to the police who retained them until they were reunited & buried with him at Retford. These items were his wallet containing a 1/6d cinema ticket, address & prayer book, most of his uniform & his well earned pilots wings. One other personal item was a ring inscribed with his surname, uncovered back in 1940 just after the crash by the salvage crew, along with his service identity tag or dog tag, as it was known.

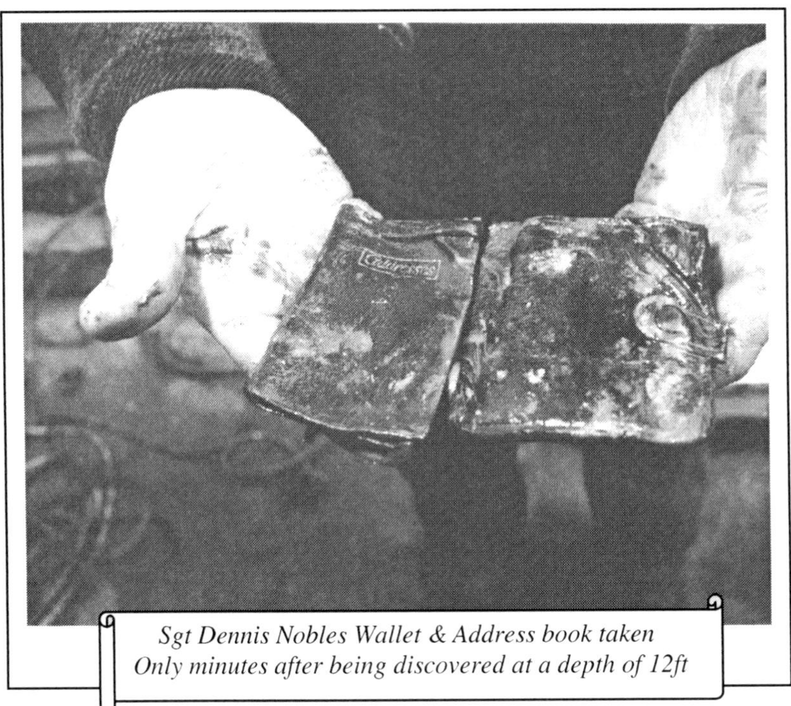

Sgt Dennis Nobles Wallet & Address book taken Only minutes after being discovered at a depth of 12ft

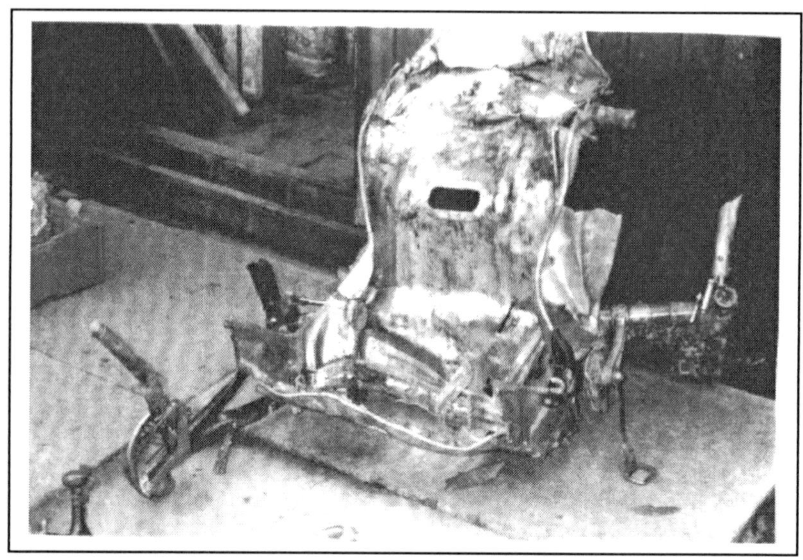

Pilots seat in which Sgt Noble was Discovered (TOP)
Compass Under carriage Release Lever, Rudder Pedal
Carburettor Butter fly & shaft, & Part of Supercharger

Hurricane P3179 undergoing restoration to museum display standard. Please note… The seat and armour plate… Also some of the original woodwork… Sgt Nobles parachute is also to be exhibited above the wreckage.

Peter Allen a new recruit to the project has spent many hours helping to prepare remnants of the Hurricane for exhibit, also assisting me with the talk & slide show designed to encourage younger generations to take an interest in British history 1940. One question still remains, who will preside over these historic artefacts in 40 or 50 years from now. The Battle of Britain is not at present a part of the education curriculum therefore how is the young generation supposed to have knowledge of perhaps the most important confrontation Britain ever faced during the 20th century. This question immediately gave me the inspiration, deciding the future of residency of Hurricane P3179. **Tangmere Aviation Museum** Sussex is dedicated to teach children of all ages the history of aviation, including the principles of flight. Apart from the fact that Hurricane P3179 is now an education in it's self. Members of the museum including myself would be pleased to continue teaching the history of aviation as & when requested.

Hurricane P3179 Exhibited with Sgt Dennis Noble's Personal Items & many Photographs

'Noble Court' is now a name associated with the townfolk of Brighton & Hove. After the reinstatement of the crash-site came another major project, building a new £2.5 million residential apartment complex on the site of the old people's home that had stood there since the 1960s & before that allotments. This magnificent structure was opened in the summer of 1998; members of the Noble family were invited to attend a ceremony & the unveiling of a plaque by Hove MP Ivor Caplin.
His Squadron denied Dennis Noble a flypast at his funeral owing to bad weather fortunately the RAF **Battle of Britain Memorial Flight** consisting of the Hurricane, Lancaster & Spitfire were able to fly overhead at roof top height directly over the crash-site, a fitting tribute in air space once taken up by Sgt Noble. Our Team feels that it played only a small part in obtaining for him the wide measure of recognition that is now his, sincere thanks must go to the media for the part they have played bringing the story to the fore. Anyone wishing to pay his or her respects to
Sgt Dennis Noble can do so in the Remembrance Garden at Tangmere Aviation Museum or St Andrews Church in the Village of Tangmere where many of the 'Few' now Rest in Peace.

"HE SHALL NOT GROW OLD"

Finally, during 1999 a Junkers Ju 87 Stuka engine plus radiator & other wreckage became snarled in the fishing nets of a trawler & were taken to Tangmere Aviation Museum & are exhibited alongside Sgt Noble's Hurricane. Upon receiving the Map co-ordination from the fishermen we discovered it coincided to an area described in a Combat Report filed by Sgt Noble on August 16th 1940 after shooting down a German Junkers Ju 87 Stuka approximately one mile off Selsey Bill, a very close proximity indeed. Identification numbers are being checked & it appears highly probable at this stage, this is the German dive-bomber destroyed by Dennis Noble after attacking Tangmere Airfield.
"*Details of reported action*" **3/St G2 Junkers Ju87B** shot down into the sea at 1300hrs by 43 Squadron aircraft, **Uffz P Bohn** & **Obergefr J Bader** both picked up by RAF Launch unhurt.

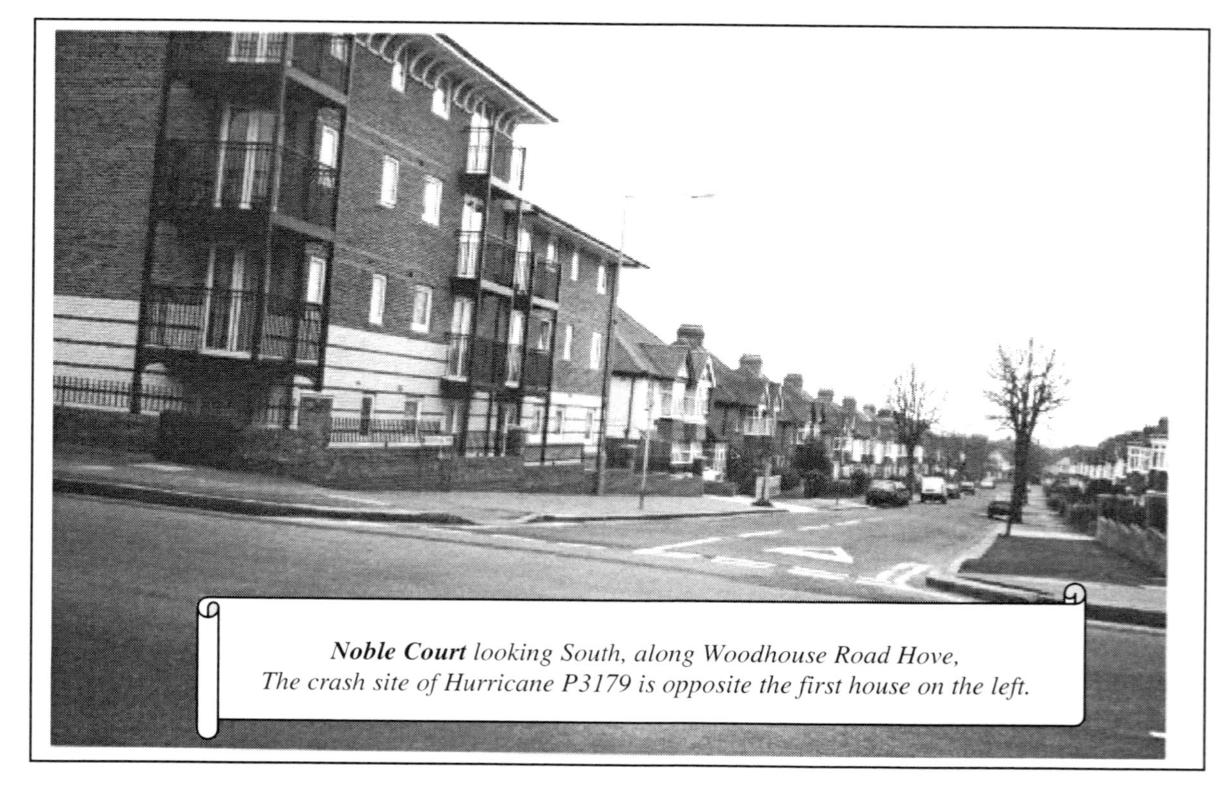

***Noble Court** looking South, along Woodhouse Road Hove,*
The crash site of Hurricane P3179 is opposite the first house on the left.

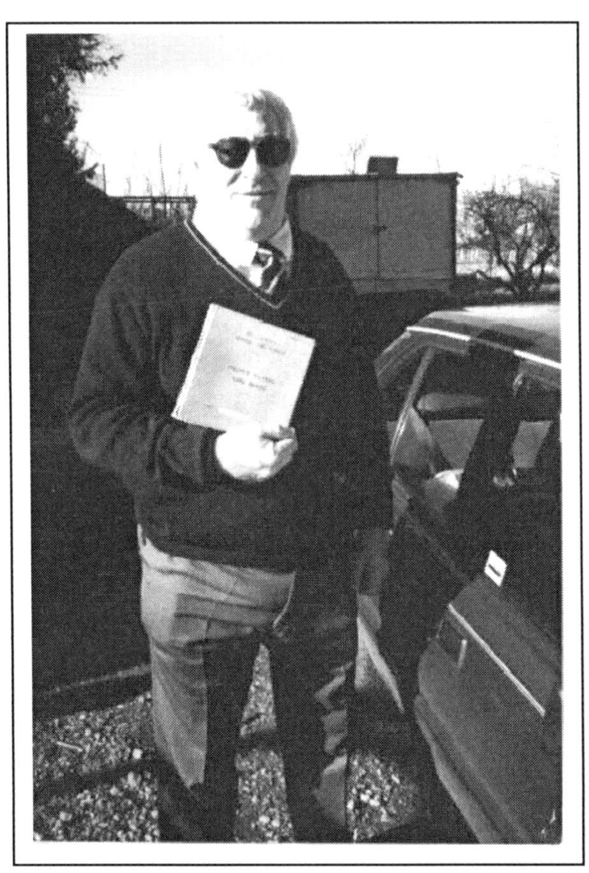

Denis Noble Junior.
Holding Sgt Nobles Log Book

EPILOGUE.

Contributed by the Reverend Anthony Martlew.

"I am privileged to have been able to write this Epilogue, for me it concludes a deeply moving experience, which commenced Friday 30th August 1940". As a twelve-year-old schoolboy my interest in what was happening around me during WW2 was intense. Everything pertaining to aerial combat was particularly high on my list, I knew where every aircraft Allied or German had crashed within a 20-mile radius of my home, my bedroom window was littered with souvenirs taken from many crash-sites.
On that day my father & I were watching the engagement overhead & we both saw a Hurricane in a vertical dive to the south of us, my mother was a stickler for punctuality – especially where mealtimes were concerned & was adamant that I should not immediately get onto my bike to rush to the scene of a crash. I remembered a rather hurried meal & escaped as quickly as possible to where I thought the Hurricane to be. I located it with out any trouble & was confronted by a crater surrounded by an enormous mound of golden brown clay. Spectators told me that the pilots body had been recovered but the engine was buried to deep to be excavated. Even as the years passed, I began to doubt whether more fragments could have been found that day.
When in August 1996 I learned from the local press that an attempt was to be made to recover P3179 – the aircraft that I had seen crashing, I felt I should become involved. I did have something practical to offer having seen the original crater. I contacted Keith Arnold & we visited the site together. On the day of the dig I scoured the pile of clay removed by the JCB Excavator with a metal detector for any small objects left undiscovered by the team. On the second day Saturday **November 9th 1996** that the remains of Sgt Dennis Noble were discovered, for all of us it was a very emotional experience & I shall never forget the look on Keith's face as he held Sgt Noble's Wallet in his hand.
In my ministry as a Hospice Chaplain I deal with death & grieving

Relatives on a regular basis, but this where outside any spiritual experience that I had previously encountered. The feeling of Dennis's presence was overwhelming. I was not the only one to feel this for one of the team working in the excavation (which was then about 12 feet in depth) appeared at the top of the ladder looking very pale & saying that he couldn't go back down the hole as he had heard a voice in his head which kept saying to him "For God's sake get me out of here".

The next day was Remembrance Sunday & it had been arranged to hold a service at the site. By midday a large crowd had gathered – the British Legion & members of a local ATC Squadron also TV crews & members of the public.

As I began the service on that bleak November day, standing next to Dennis's open parachute a wonderful sense of peace descended on us all. It was as though Dennis was saying that our task of removing his remains from there & allowing him to rest in his hometown, was indeed the right thing to have done.

It has been suggested by some that it was morally wrong to disturb him & that the dig should never have taken place. There are a number of factors to consider least the fact that Dennis had been lying directly under the trade's entrance to a building. Delivery lorries & vans had been constantly running over the site; that alone in my view was a valid reason to remove his remains to a proper grave. One member of the team had admitted to no pretence of belief in any thing spiritual but was deeply affected by the service. He later admitted that it had been the first time that he felt there was more to life than material things.

It is also interesting to note that during the 1960s a Council run rest home was built immediately north east of the crash-site. This has now made way for the new building NOBLE COURT.

I have spoken to an ex-member of staff at the rest home **Tessa Wakeham** who had some strange experiences while working there. Both she & a blind resident heard & felt a presence when no one else was in the room with them. Another resident **Dolly?** Saw a man in uniform who in her room twice before

& on one occasion had sat on the edge of her bed, & then suddenly disappeared. Yet another resident **Mrs Grippa,** now deceased saw an airman walk straight through her bedroom wall several times. It is interesting that at least four people felt no alarm at this presence. I shall not endeavour to explain these incidents; only leave them to your thoughts, but these visitations, if that is what we may call them have only served to strengthen my belief that we released an unhappy Spirit from an undesirable place.

May God be with you Dennis - you did not die in vain.

"Requiescat in pace."

Revd, Anthony Martlew

Planes from a Logbook.

The Vital Statistics.

De Havilland DH 60 Gipsy Moth.

Sgt Noble began his career in the Royal Air Force at Redhill Aerodrome, Surrey, making his first debut flight in the DH 60 Moth Biplane; designed during the 1920s it became a first class training aircraft without standing abilities. The DH 60 was later upgraded & renamed the TIGER MOTH or DH82A an aircraft that almost everyone living close to a country airfield would see gracing the skies on a fine summer's day. Sgt Dennis Noble's first flights were in **K1118, K1852 & K1884** during 1938.

Specifications

Wing Span 30 feet.
Overall Length 23 feet 11 inches.
Wing area 243 square feet.
Weight empty 900 lbs loaded 1400lbs
Power unit 120 hp Gipsy11

Tiger Moth T7694 Taken during 1944.

Miles Magister M14a.

Dennis flew fourteen different Magisters throughout his training between November 1938 & July 1939, these aircraft were all based at Redhill Aerodrome, Surrey. **L8335, L8336, L8342, N3039, N3738, N3782, N3783, N3792, N3793, N3803, N3805, N3812, N3837, N3842 & N3843** Dennis flew N3792 on November 5th 1938 with instructor Flt Dale & with his very last flight in the Magister L3843 with Flt Lovell on his test.
The Magister entered RAF service 1937 eventually being replaced by the De Havilland Chipmunk in the late 40s, it was a competent little plane used for operational duties dispatching communications to RAF EFTS units & perfect for training pilots giving them the thrills of flying a mono wing rather than the ageing biplanes. Many Magisters were purchased after the war & continued to fly, this time in civilian service. There are only a few left today of which one belongs to shuttle worth collection P6382, a second T9738 is at Breighton Selby, the third T9707 is at the Science Museum, Manchester with a fourth at the Imperial War Museum, Duxford Cambridge.

Specifications.

Wing span 33 ft 10 inches
Length 25ft 3inches
Monologue box with spruce longerons
& covered in a plywood skin,
Vacuum operated flaps,
Fixed undercarriage,
Powered by a 130 hp De Havilland Gypsy Major
Four cylinder inverted engine of 6124cc.
Service ceiling was 1800 feet.

Hawker Hart & the Hawker Audax.

In 1932 the Audax became one of the RAFs first training planes with dual controls, basically it was a Hawker Hart, the rear gunners position having been moved to make way for the extra cockpit area. A biplane of outstanding manoeuvrability that eventually paved the way to the design of the Hurricane, it had polished silver alloy panels that covered the Rolls-Royce Kestrel V12 engine producing 510 horse power, the training version was 525hp producing a top speed of 165mph for the Hart & 170mph for the Audax.
Dennis piloted Hart Numbers **K4758, K4762, K4942, K4968, K4982, K5021, K5024, K5784, K6465, K6484, K6496, K6508, K6511, K6539, K6540 & K6805.** The Audax's were **K2001, K3101, K3698, K3707, K4402, K4405, K5133, K5211, K5215, K5216, K6496, K7320, K7327, K7402, K7407, K7414, K7417, K7440, K7500, and K8316.** Dennis piloted his first Hart K6540 July 1939 & his first Audax K2001, 13th July 1939.

Hawker Audax K3718 at Hawkinge 1935

North American TEXAN T6 or HARVARD,

Dennis was given the chance to fly this beautiful aeroplane at 6. O. T. U Sutton Bridge training establishment. This was a step in the right direction towards his ultimate goal, taking the controls of a Hurricane or Spitfire, the RAF's latest fighting machines.

Spent 55 minutes practicing circuits & landings on the 8th July 1940. Under dual instruction with **P/O Lewis** & another 50 minutes flying solo in **Harvard L7176,** he would soon have grasped the characteristics of this fine aircraft in flight. Dennis progressed to the Hurricane after these short flights, but still had other chances to fly the Harvard. His next was **L7175** acting as a target for gunnery practice July 19th 1940 & again in L7176 as safety pilot on the 23rd July, the other pilot accompany him was his chum **Sgt A. L. M Deller** who had joined 43 Squadron with Dennis on the 3rd August. Sgt, Deller survived two brushes from death during the Battle of Britain, one a forced landing at Tangmere 12th August 1940 & another on September 7th after baling out of his Hurricane V7309 finally crashing at Babylon farm, Sutton Valence. Sgt, Deller retired from the RAF in 1946 to live in America.

The RAF & the Royal Canadian Air Force both knew the Texan as the Harvard. First produced in 1939 as the AT-6 & powered by a Pratt & Whitney 600hp Wasp radial engine, although designed as a trainer it could be adapted to carry bombs or rockets under the wings. There are many Harvard's still operating throughout the world & hopefully, for many years to come.

This amazing aeroplane can be heard approaching by its distinct beating sound created by the propeller tips as they travel in close proximity to the speed of sound, automatically turning ones head skywards in admiration to all those lucky enough to have flown it.

Specifications,

Cruising speed of 146-mph. Top speed was 209 mph.

Length 29 feet, Height 11 feet 8 inches.

Weight 42711 lbs empty. Total weight 5617 lbs

Mile's Master Advanced Trainer,

Flying Instructors cherished this aircraft as it gave them chance to teach pupils what it would be like to fly the Hurricane or Spitfire. The characteristics were almost identical even the cockpit layout was similar. It was a fast aeroplane with a max. speed of 250 miles per hour giving the pilot his first taste of high speed flying.
This aircraft also had a unique retractable undercarriage that turned & retracted backwards before entering the wings. Dennis flew **N7804,** July 26th 1940 at Sutton Bridge for 50 minutes experience on type.

Specifications,

Powered by a 585hp Rolls-Royce Kestrel XXX,
Some were fitted with a Bristol Mercury Radial engine.
Low wing cantilever monoplane,
Constructed of wood.

****

Fairey Battle,
Dennis flew this remarkably clumsy fighter-bomber twice; the first time was **N7378,** on July 22nd 1940 with **P/O Forrester**. Their task was to observe aerial attacks. The second flight was on July28th, flying solo to gain experience on the type lasting for duration of one hour five minutes.
Although powered by the Rolls-Royce 1030hp Merlin II engine, it proved a very slow & clumsy aeroplane owing to power to weight ratio. Although vastly underpowered it could still carry a bomb load of 1000 to 1500Ib almost equalling the German Junkers 87 Stuka. Fairey Battles were sent over the channel to bomb invasion barges in being assembled in French Harbours such as Calais or Boulogne, but its pilots had to be careful not to tangle with German fighters, as the Fairey Battle would be outclassed even though it carried machine guns that were more effective for strafing ground targets. Although one of the RAF's medium bombers, powers that be decided to keep it back for training or target towing which it was ideally suited.

Hawker Hurricane Mk1,

One word describing this trusted workhorse or gun platform would be 'Castle'. Not only did it have the firepower its defences for the occupant were robust. Built with a steel tubular design similar to that of the Sopwith Camel & Hawker Fury. Basically a box section steel frame with bracing wires, wooden formers & stringers then covered with fabric, proving to be a knight in shining armour to many pilots after horrific battle damage. It was not unknown for Hurricanes returning home to have pieces of tail missing or gaping holes in the wings, leaving ground staff bewildered as to 'how' an aeroplane could fly with such damage, the pilot possibly shaken but ready & able to fight another day. They were strong & easy to repair but without the talents of Sir Sidney Camm & his team at Hawkers in 1937, this fine aircraft would not have been a success. Britain managed to mass-produce the Hurricane with the first batch of 600, making their first flights on 12th October 1937. One of these consignments was **L1548** issued to 111 Squadron Northholt, & eventually transferred to 6 O.T.U. Sutton Bridge. This happened to be Dennis's first Hurricane his dream becoming reality on 8th July 1940 when he made his first flight in this aeroplane. Another was **L1714.** This eventually went to 79 squadron Biggin Hill, Kent in December 1937 also finding its way to Sutton Bridge training establishment, as did **L1924** after spending time with 3 Squadron, Kenley. 43 Squadron were allocated **L1736 on** 30th December 1938 where it remained with them until 16th August 1940 when a glycol leak caused it to catch fire whilst in the charge of P/O Crisp who baled out of the machine before it crashed into the sea.

Dennis flew Hurricane **L1739** on 6th August 1940, his first since joining 43 Squadron, logged as 'Formation practice.' This aircraft was destroyed on the 15th August with P/O Montgomery being killed 40 miles off Beachy Head, Sussex. **L1836** started its career with 504 Squadron at Hucknell & then onto 32 Squadron, Biggin Hill before joining 43 Squadron & was subsequently damaged in a forced landing at Ford Aerodrome, Sussex, but was kept in storage awaiting repair where it was eventually converted to a MkII during 1941. Hurricane **V7221** was built by Hawker at Kingston Langley, 1940, then transferred from 43 Squadron to 213 squadron, 29th October 1940.**V7366** went to 59 O.T.U & converted to a sea Hurricane as a MkII. Hurricanes listed in Sgt nobles Logbook are as follows... **L1548, L1714, L1736** FT-H Sgt Crisp baled out from this aircraft 16th August 1940 (write off). **L1739** Sgt Noble was posted as missing in this aircraft 15th August 1940, in fact force landed at Ford aerodrome. **L1836, L1924, L2006, L2073, N2469, N2647, P3179 & P3466** FT-X transferred to Drem January 1941. **P3619, P3903, V7221, V7321, & V7366** Not any of these Hurricanes survive today intact. Hurricane **P3179** was built by Gloster Aircraft Ltd under license number 96237 & was one of the first to be fitted with the three bladed Rotol propeller, discovered on a fragment of plywood from behind the seat was the date 16th February 1940 plus the remains of two faded signatures. P3179 was fitted with the Rolls-Royce Merlin III engine & was for some reason stored until 8th August 1940 then delivered to 43 squadron Tangmere. P3179s first Test flight for its Airworthiness certificate was under taken by **Flt lt Dalton Morgan** 11th August. Other flights recorded by squadron pilots were...

12th " " " " **P/O Roy du Vivier 10.35 -11.55 hrs**
13th " " " " **P/O Van den Hove 14.15 -15.00 16.05 - 1645**
14th " " " " **P/O Roy du Vivier ------ 18.05 – 19.30**

16th August 1940 **Squadron leader Tubby Badger** flew P3179 into battle against Junkers Ju 87 Stukas that attacked Tangmere Airfield destroying three. One of the Stukas from 3/StG2 crashed on the B2145 Selsey road nr the Junction of Church Norton Uffz E Konig & Uffz J Schmidt were captured badly injured. Badger flew P3179 on one more occasion 18th August 1940. One other pilot who flew this favorable mount was **P/O Gorrie** on the 25th August 1940 at 06.15 – 06.35 possibly a test flight in readiness for the days action.

Specifications.

HURRICANE Mk1.

Wing span 40 feet,
Length 31ft 6ins.
Weight 4670lbs – 6600lbs fully loaded,
Powered by 1,030 hp Rolls-Royce Merlin II later III
V12 liquid cooled engine,
Three Blade constant speeds Rotol, or Watts 2 bladed wooden propeller.
Range of 730 miles,
Duration 3.5 hours
Top Speed 330 mph,
Ceiling 35,000 feet,
Armament Eight 303 Browning machine-guns four in each wing.

Hawker Hurricane MkII ***LF738***
At Biggin Hill during 1965.Built 1943/44

RETFORD & DISTRICT SPITFIRE.

Retford Town, Nottinghamshire, has been excellent & providing commendable examples of devoted individual acts of heroism throughout British history. One such achievement was in 1620 when many of the townsfolk joined the Mayflower expedition to the Americas, not forgetting the soldiers, sailors & airmen who gave their lives for the freedom of their beloved Town in Two World Wars.

The thought of being invaded during World War II united the people together once again. This time they decided to raise funds towards the purchase of an urgently required Spitfire for the RAF. Eventually enough funding was raised to buy Spitfire R7218 bearing its commemorative plaque *Retford & District.*

Built by Vickers Armstrong at Castle Bromwich as an Mk1 then converted to an MkV, It was delivered to No 38 Maintenance Unit on the 21st March 1941. After a few days, it was operational with 611 Squadron at Rochford, now more widely recognized as Southend Aerodrome. After a few weeks R7218 was transferred to 145 Squadron at Merston & two days later whilst on operations it was shot down crashing in flames, the pilot being Flying Officer **Machacek** a Czechoslovakian who was flying one of ten aircraft on patrol to Lille in France.

Early in the afternoon at 14.35 hrs, ten aircraft took off from Merston, on a Circus. Three returned just before reaching the French coast, the remainder continued on Patrol but became separated from each other whilst taking evasive action, F/O Machacek & P/O **Ping** failed to return.

R7218 crashed in flames in the garden of M.Rene Bonte in Mores. An I.D. Disc was discovered by M. Bonte inscribed with F/O Machaceks details as was subsequently confiscated by the Germans. A grave was prepared in the cemetery at Adinkerkes, except that for reasons unknown the German authorities sent the pilot's body to Bruges for burial.

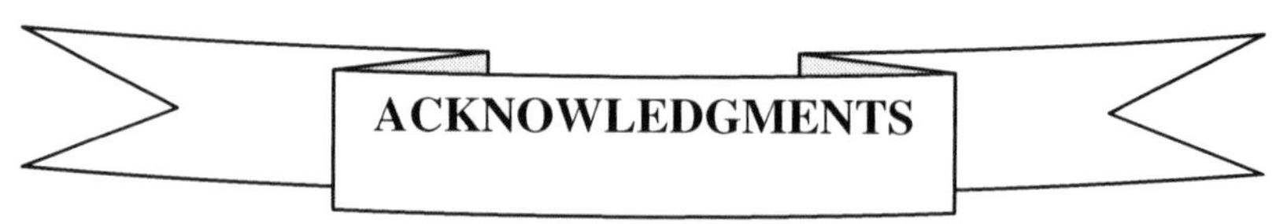

ACKNOWLEDGMENTS

KEITH ARNOLD (Author) wishes to express thanks to the following, for their help & patience during the compiling of this book & to the many helpers involved in the project.
Also my wife June for her patients & help whilst compiling this book
With a special thanks to the Excavation Team.

Southern Counties Aviation Club,

TEAM MEMBERS

Keith Arnold, Aviation Archaeologist & Project Co-ordinator.
June " " Project Administration Secretary.
Trevor " " Building Supervisor, Carpentry & Plumbing
Arnold Family, Charmaine, Melanie, Keith Jnr & Simon
Keith Boniface, Site Security Officer.
Martin Reilly, Photographer.
Peter Watson, " "
Graham Smith, Recovery Team
Jamie Earley, " "
Mike Mountford, " "
Rev Tony Martlew, A true & valid member & eyewitness 1940.
Cyril & Rose Linter, Thanks for the support & refreshments.
Tony Diamond, British Telecom Supervisor.
Colin Southouse, Highways Supervisor.
Peter Watson Team member during cleaning operations.
Mark Butler, 'Stone Mason' for his assistance.
With special thanks to **David Brocklehurst** from the
(Kent Battle of Britain Museum, Hawkinge, Kent.)
Colin Lee Croydon Aviation Research Group.

Acknowledgments Continued,

176, Squadron, Hove, Crowd & Traffic Control.
The **Royal Air Force** Recovery Team from ST Athan Wales.
Ministry of Defence Innsworth.
RAF 43 Squadron at Leuchars, Scotland.
RAF 51 " Waddington for organising the internment 1997
RAF Battle of Britain Memorial Flight for flypast, at the opening ceremony of Noble Court.
RAF Hendon, for their assistance throughout the project.
John Thorpe for his valid assistance with this book.
Not forgetting **Browns Haulage Contractors** for the kind use of the Excavators, lorries & Materials.
John Milham for the Mini Digger signs & his expertises
Staff of **Tangmere Military Aviation Museum** in particular **Ken Murch** for his professional assistance displaying Hurricane P3179.

Group Captain Tom Dalton-Morgan DSO. OBE. DFC. B Sc. BE.
Group Captain Frank Carey CBE, DFC, AFC, DFM & American Silver Star, for his help with the research.
Group Captain George Westlake 43 Squadron, DSO, DFC.
Wing Commander N.P.W Hancock OBE, DFC,
Sgt, AG Russell, of 43 Squadron 1940.
Bill Littlemore, 43 Squadron 'B' Flight ground crew 1940.
Bill Topping
Bill Taylor for photographs of Retford & other information.
Norman Ingle.
Paul Kendle Owner of 59 Wood house Road Hove.
Roy Humphrey's Author of the book Hawkinge, for supplying photographs of Audax, DH 60 Moth & Hurricane.

Ken Lowe. Research information.
Les Cherriman Chichester Diocesan Housing Association.
Ian Douglas for information & photograph of Sqdn Ldr Badger.
Dr J Gooding J.P & HM Coroner.
Revd Martin Loveless, 51 Squadron Chaplain Waddington.
Revd John Watts

Credit must also be given to the dedicated helpers who have given up their spare time supporting this project.

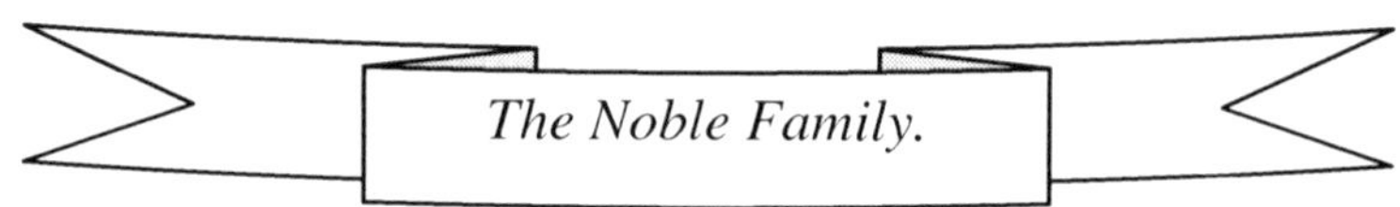

John Noble. Dennis's elder Brother.
Mrs Evans, formally Mrs John Noble.
Denis Noble Junior.
George & Gwendolyn Noble.
Mrs Ethel Knight.
Florence Chayter
Vera Cywinski.
Mrs D Scott.

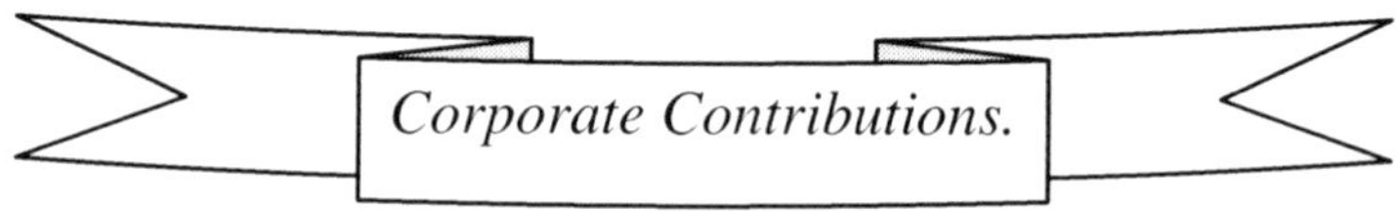

BBC Southern Counties Radio
BBC Radio Nottingham
BBC Television.
Yorkshire Television
Meridian Television
Barry Coding Photography.
Evening Argus

Express Printing Crawley Sussex,
International News papers,
Retford Times,
Retford & Bawtrey Guardian,
Shoreham Herald,
British Library,
Hove Records Office
Public Records Office Kew, London,
Lewes Public Records Office Sussex,
Science Museum London
Protective Textile Company,
Sussex Fire Brigade,
Sussex Police,
RAF Museum Hendon,
Beaumont Publications (43 Squadron by J Beedle)
Basset Law Council, Nottingham,
Brighton & Hove Council,
East Sussex County Council,
West Sussex County Council,
Scotland Yard,
Chichester Diocesan Housing Association,
Brenzett Aviation Museum,
The Kent Battle of Britain Museum Hawkinge,
The Battle of Britain Fighter Association,
R.A.F.A Hove Branch,
With Special Thanks to John Thorpe.

BBC South Documentary "Requiem for an Airfield, Tangmere" 1985.

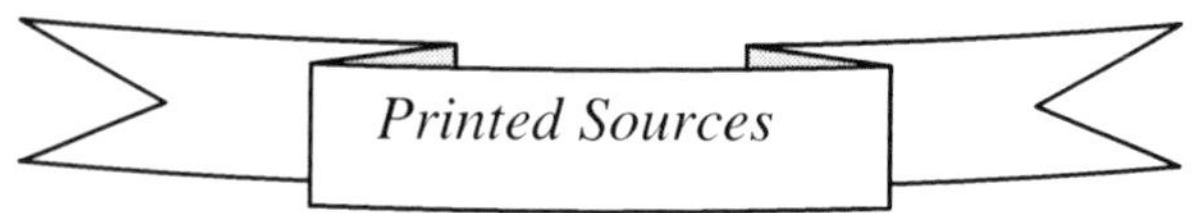

J Beedle 43(F) Squadron Beaumont Aviation Literature 1966,
Battle of Britain Then & Now Humphrey Wynn
Publishers Battle of Britain Prints 3, Plaistow Road London,
Men of the Battle of Britain, Kenneth Wynn Gliddon Books 1989,
D.L Murray Brighton & Hove in Battle Dress, 1939-45
Brighton Herald Ltd 1946,

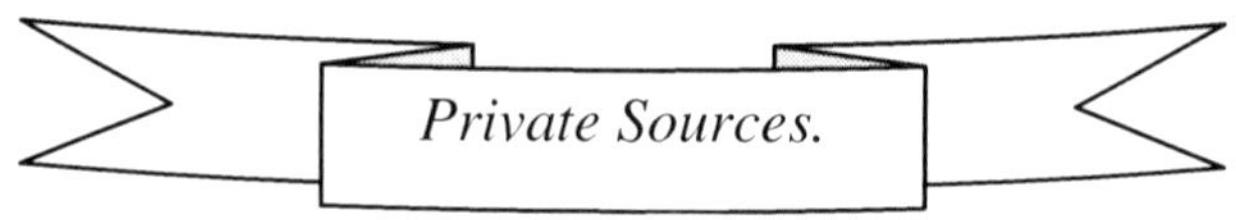

Letters to Author
Combat reports JVC Badger. DFC. 1940,
Interview & Letters Group Captain, Frank Carey.
DFM. DFC & 2 bars. AFC. CBE.
Foreword by Group Captain, T.F.Dalton-Morgan.
DSO. OBE.DFC.
Mrs A.R Evans,
John Noble,
Denis Noble Jnr,
George & Gwendolyn Noble,
Rev John Watts,
Rev Tony Martlew.
Sgt Dennis Nobles own Pilots Log Book.
The Ulster Aviation Society.

A Special thanks to those who contributed
Research Material.

TRIBUTES,

The Author wishes to pay tribute to those no longer with us, who have given a great deal towards this Project.

REST IN PEACE

JOAN ARNOLD.
JOHN NOBLE.
Rev JOHN WATTS
Sgt Bill LITTLEMORE
KEN LOWE
ANNIE EVANS

43 Squadron (The Fighting Cocks)

F/Sgt KM Allen, Fl M.R Atkinson, Sgt CAH Ayling, Sqdn Ldr JVC Badger, Sgt HJR Barrow, Sgt HE Bennet, Sgt V Brejcha, P/O GC Brunner, Sgt JA Buck, P/O F Carey, F/O MK Carswell, P/O RI Chaffe, Sgt JL Crisp, P/O Cruttenden, Sgt V Cukr, Sgt ALM Deller, P/O DG Gorrie, P/O CK Gray, F/O B Groszewski, P/O EN Gunter, P/O HJL Hallowes, F/O Hawdrth, F/L CB Hull, Sgt CAL Hurry, Sgt G Jefferson, Sgt GW Jeffery's, P/O EW Jereczek, Sgt ER Jessop, Sgt RA Johnson, Flt JI Kilmartin,P/O R Lane, P/O EC Langdon, P/O Darg Leroy du Vivier, P/O KW Mackenzie, Sgt B Malinowski, Sgt JP Mills, Sgt H Montgomery, Flt TFD Morgan, Sgt JP Morrison, P/O K Mrazek, Sgt D Noble, F/O HL North, P/O JRS Oelofse, Sgt GCC Palliser, Sgt J Pipa, Sgt R Ptacek, P/O J Redman, Flt RC Reynell, Sgt AG Russell, F/O LH Schwind, Sgt Sika, Flt JWC Simpson, F/O J Stenhouse, Sgt GR Stoodly, Sgt LV Toogood, Sgt FJ Twitchett, P/O HC Upton, P/O Van den Hove, P/O GH Westlake, P/O CA Woods-Scawen.

Flight Commanders 1940,

Sqdn Ldr G Lott November 1939 to July 1940,
" " J.V.C. Badger July to August 1940
" " C.B Hull August to September 1940,
" T.F.D Morgan September to October 1941

Authors Comment.

'It has given me immense pleasure portraying the life of Sgt Dennis Noble, who has been the topic of conversation in many households throughout the country. I have been asked numerous questions over the past few years the main one being 'How or Why' was he left still in the Cockpit of his Hurricane? I can only explain the evidence from my research that has taken almost six years to complete, & hope I have achieved enlightening the younger generation of the Courage & Bouts of Heroism young flyers such as Dennis gave towards Freedom & Democracy. My research has brought Dennis Noble close to my heart & his knowledge has revealed to me how it was all those years ago. I am now more acquainted with his existence than my own brother's today. I hope this project educates younger generations who need to gain knowledge of the Battle of Britain & what it has meant to generations since. "At present it is still not taught in the Schools curriculum, could this be a fraction of our history that has progressively elapsed"! Finally I hope that schools will take up the challenge & Visit the Display of Hurricane P3179 at Tangmere Military Aviation Museum Sussex where this story began.

Keith Arnold.

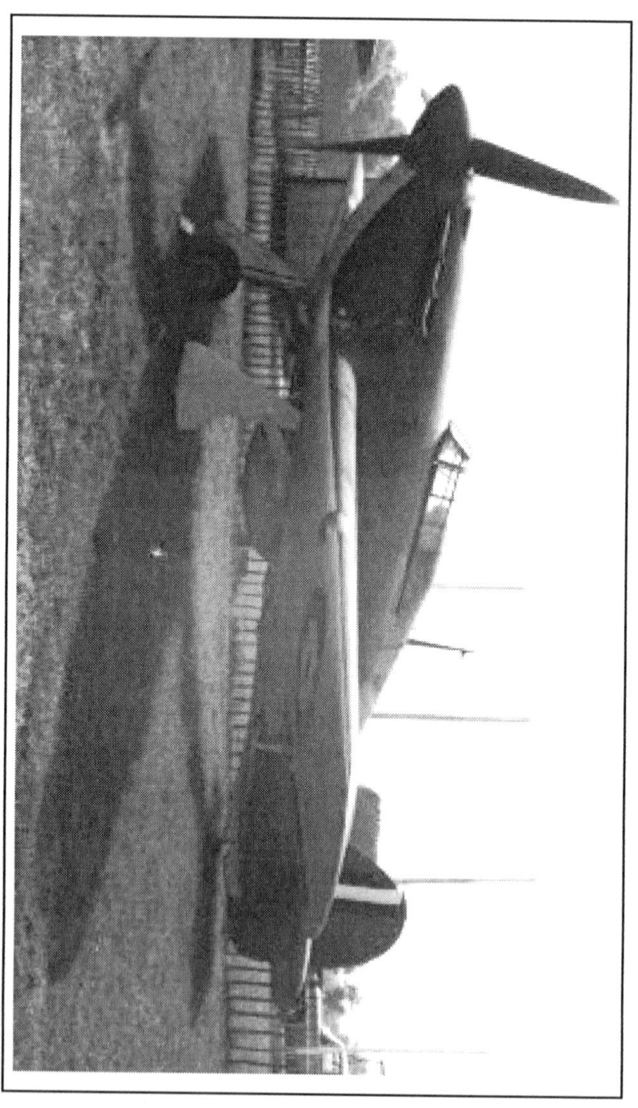